Your Church Can Thrive

HAROLD PERCY

Your Church Can Thrive

Making the Connections that Build Healthy Congregations

Abingdon Press
Nashville

YOUR CHURCH CAN THRIVE
MAKING THE CONNECTIONS THAT BUILD HEALTHY CONGREGATIONS

This book is printed on acid-free paper.

Library of Congress Cataloging-in-Publication Data

Percy, Harold.
    Your church can thrive : making the connections that build
healthy congregations / Harold Percy.
        p. cm.
    ISBN 0-687-02256-8 (alk. paper)
    1. Church growth.   I. Title.

    BV652.25.P465 2003
    254'.5—dc22

                                                    2003016755

Scripture quotations, unless otherwise noted, are taken from the *Holy Bible: New International Version®*, Copyright © 1973, 1978, 1984 by the International Bible Society. Used by permission of Zondervan Publishing House. All rights reserved.

The Scripture quotation marked KJV is from the King James or Authorized Version of the Bible.

03 04 05 06 07 08 09 10 11 12—10 9 8 7 6 5 4 3 2 1

To Diane Toycen, whose vision, faith, loyalty, wise counsel, talent, and hard work over the past 15 years have been invaluable. Without you, Trinity Anglican Church, Streetsville, would not be the thriving congregation it is today. I thank you for your ministry, and I thank God for you.

CONTENTS

FOREWORD

L ook deep within your heart. Look into the eyes of the board members at your next meeting. Watch the behavior of church members at your next meeting. When was the last time you heard a church leader speak *optimistically* about the future of your congregation?

I ask this question especially of the 80-90 percent of congregations that worship fewer than 100 people. When was the last time you heard a church leader truly and sincerely express optimism about the future of your congregation that was not exaggerated expectations because the Bishop was to be in attendance, not positive thinking because you were about to launch a stewardship campaign, not sentimental hopefulness to comfort the longtime veterans attending the annual meeting, and not wishful thinking that got the personnel committee past conflict and recriminations?

Harold Percy is one of the few remaining, seriously credible optimists in congregational ministry today. This simple, straightforward, gentle book provides the reasons for such optimism. It is possible to grow a church with integrity and multiply Christian mission with power. Harold and the congregation with whom he follows Jesus are doing it in a region more estranged from church and Christ than most areas of North America. If they can do it there, you can do it in your area.

Harold's message is relevant for any church, but especially those churches that are more than 25 years old, worship fewer than 100 people, or are stuck at about 250 members growing older by the day. Also, churches with 3,000 members and only

600 in worship had better read this! Churches experiencing sudden demographic shifts toward Hispanic, or Asian populations had better read this!

I vividly recall an invitation to address a significant urban synod. Three "mistakes" were made that day. The first mistake was that the synod representatives requested me to be challenging, visionary, and prophetic to a synod in which many congregations have large endowments, clergy with secure stipends, and only handfuls of aging laity in attendance. The second mistake was that I took them up on it. The final mistake was that, like many church futurists, in the search for optimism, I was more blunt, challenging, and prophetic than most elected delegates cared to experience, for real optimism suggests that church decline may not really be due to the advance of secularity, the lure of other religions, the affluence of culture, or the aging of the population. If this scenario sounds familiar to denominational reformers and congregational transformers alike, you can well imagine a certain heat to the proceedings.

I like this book, however, because it "cooks" with less heat. Harold has the ability to be frighteningly optimistic without scaring people to death.

If you frequent Christian bookstores, you can see a common pattern of behavior among clergy and lay leaders. They scan shelves of books on church growth, organizational change, or lay empowerment with a perplexed and anxious look in their eyes. It all seems so complicated, daunting, and risky. By the time leaders have done all the work prescribed for church transformation, and survived all the conflict, they fear there will be little time and energy left to actually *do* any ministry! You can see the questions in their minds, Will it really work? Will it be beyond my training or powers of comprehension? Will it be beyond my strength, patience, or endurance?

Most times, they walk away from the church growth shelves. Clergy drift over to the preaching section, while laity drift over to the prayer and meditation section for a book on personal spirituality, stress reduction, or better board meetings. It seems wiser to just keep going than to divert onto a different and dangerous path.

Fortunately, this book is on the shelf. Harold convinces you that church growth is actually far simpler than you expect and much less stressful than you fear.

The strength of this book is that it identifies the three major attitude shifts that church leaders must make in order for the church to grow. Once these attitude shifts are made, complexity and anxiety disappear.

Church growth is about missiology, not ecclesiology! Congregational life is not about preserving a heritage, following a denominational polity, or taking care of friends. It's about multiplying mission, sharing a joyful experience of Jesus, and reaching out to strangers. *How* you "do church" is subordinate to *why* you "do church." There is a point to church participation, and it is not survival. It is outreach.

Church growth is about making disciples, not maintaining harmony. Christians are only mature if they live and share their faith in such a way as to draw others into relationship with Christ. Coach, educate, train, or do whatever is necessary; the primary task of church leadership is to grow up the church membership to simultaneously do good works and share the motivation for doing them.

Church growth is the result of a process, not a program. Behind all the tips and tactics (which Harold will share) lies a flow of experience. From the moment they appear at the door for the first time to the moment they first share faith with a friend, relative, coworker, or stranger, there is a flow of relationship building, gifts discernment, skills development, and mission focus. From the moment they first feel the sacrament in worship to the moment they first accompany a newcomer to the altar, there is a process of personal growth that is so rewarding they can't help but draw others into it.

Harold makes church growth remarkably simple and stress free. Make these attitude shifts in your own mind and in the hearts of your core leaders, and all the other strategies that Harold will share here become remarkably obvious and easy. You and your leaders can then focus on God's mission in the world, experience personal and spiritual growth along the way, and involve more and more people in a joy that is fulfilling their lives and blessing society.

Once your core leaders make these attitude shifts, the practical strategies to follow up on visiting strangers and to reach out to friends, family, and neighbors will seem remarkably noncontroversial. They will inspire you to go out of your way to be sensitive to the public God loves so much. They will stimulate you to be even more innovative in designing mission for your own local context.

Harold himself has done everything he talks about in this book and successfully coached others to do it as well. He is probably not the stereotype so many people have of a "church growth leader." He does not fit the image of the extreme extrovert, magnetic personality, media manipulator, or organizational guru. He is sensitive, positive, modest, ironic, and deeply appreciative of anyone who can bring strength to his shortcomings. More important, he is focused on mission, self-disciplined about his spiritual life, open to providence, and in love with Christ. Harold is one of the most optimistic, determined, humorous, and *ordinary* church leaders I know.

Many church leaders use their stereotype of a church growth leader as a tool to excuse their own inaction. They tell themselves they either cannot be this way or do not want to be this way, and so they use their very inaction as a sign of some mythical integrity. It is not hard to imagine Peter, James, John (or Priscilla or Lydia), or other apostles from New Testament times trying to pull off the same deception. Today, as then, Christ is undeceived.

I can imagine Jesus encountering you in the deserted vestry, or the quiet sanctuary, or the business board meeting, as he met Peter in the customary surroundings of beach, boat, and sea. Three times he says to "Simon, son of John," Do you love me more than property, program, and ceremony? Do you love me more than balanced budgets and membership privileges? Do you love me more than peaceful meetings, predictable strategic plans, and preserving the status quo?

Then, as now, leaders like you can say, "Yes, Lord, you know that I love you!" That's all it takes to begin church growth. Christ can take over and do the rest.

THOMAS G. BANDY

INTRODUCTION

M y purpose in writing this book is to help congregations (perhaps especially congregations of the so-called mainline denominations) become more effective in connecting with people currently outside of church life and a vital Christian faith in order to influence them with the gospel.

Many mainline congregations have ambivalent feelings about church growth. My experience in many years of working with churches in Canada and the United States is that most congregations would like to grow, but at the same time they don't want to get caught up in what many refer to as "the numbers game." I think what they are trying to say is that they want growth with integrity. This book seeks to address this issue.

Another difficulty that many congregations face is that they have no real idea of how to think about growth in a strategic way or how to focus their energies and prioritize their activities and resources so that they might be able to grow.

In this book I identify four distinct categories of people whom a typical church can influence and offer some thoughts on what a church might do in order to be able to connect with people in each of these categories. But before thinking about these categories and how to reach them, chapter 1 deals with the issue of growth in general and raises the question of why churches might want to grow in the first place. There are both good and bad reasons for wanting to do so.

I offer this book with the prayer that clergy and congregational leaders who desire to become more effective in connecting with outsiders for the sake of the gospel might find it both an encouragement and a practical help. May God bless you in your important ministry of nurturing into existence communities of ordinary people learning to live to the glory of God. There is no more important work in the whole world than this.

CHAPTER ONE

THINKING ABOUT GROWTH

All across North America there are congregations that would love to be able to grow. My purpose in writing this book is to help them. But before we get into the practical issues of how churches can grow, it is important to ask some questions about why they should want to. In congregational life, as in many other endeavors, the question *why* should always precede the question *how*.

On the surface this might seem a rather curious suggestion. It doesn't really require an astute observer to see that many congregations are dwindling numerically. Many church members who are interested in the future of the church (or at least of their own congregation) comment that we had better do something about recruiting new members because the current ones are dying off or dropping out at an alarming rate and the prospects for the future aren't looking too good.

> *In congregational life, the question* why *should always precede the question* how.

Still others remark that of course we want to attract new members because those of us who have been here for many years are growing tired and need more hands to help with the work of keeping this place going. Or they observe that finances are tight, and it surely would help if we could recruit some new members to help pay the bills. Sometimes, in more formal church language, this is referred to as the need to build up the financial base or increase the number of "giving units." One church consultant wryly remarked that most of the churches he was dealing with were operating on a model of congregational development that he had dubbed "the vampire model." "Everywhere I go," he remarked, "people are commenting that what their congregation needs is some new blood!"

There is also the matter of looking successful. It is usually not much fun being part of a dwindling congregation. Obviously, it would be more enjoyable to be part of one that is growing and thriving. Perhaps for clergy in particular, issues of self-image, perceived competence, and morale are involved here. Many sense that they would find their work more fulfilling and feel better about themselves if only they could attract some new members through their ministry.

All of these are valid issues; perhaps they are even compelling reasons to put some serious effort into attracting new members. But in the end they all appear to be self-serving. They are all motivated by what this congregation or what this leader needs in order to keep going. Somewhere there is a nudge of uneasiness that there must be more to it; after all, isn't the gospel about serving rather than being served? Some troublesome thinkers in the congregation may even wonder out loud, "Is the community here to help the church, or is the church here to help the community?"

A Couple of Radical Questions

Someone once observed that the most radical question any organization can ask itself is, Why are we doing what we are doing? The second most radical question is, Why are we doing it the way we are doing it? When a congregation, for whatever reason, begins to get serious about growth, these are certainly among the first questions it should ask. They are absolutely foundational.

Why are we doing what we are doing? Why are we doing it the way we are doing it?

It is an interesting fact that many (I would even dare to say most) congregations have not asked these questions in a long time. It never occurs to them to do so. They go on, year after year, coming to worship; sitting on committees; making decisions about buildings, and finances, and programs without ever asking, What is all this supposed to be accomplishing? What is the bottom line that all of these activities and expenditures are seeking to realize? To put it somewhat more bluntly, at some point we need to raise the question, What business are we in?

This is an intriguing track to go down, because it leads us to the bedrock question of what it means to be the church. Assuming that the church is God's idea (and without this conviction there is hardly any good reason for being involved with the church), the questions become, Why does God want there to be a church in the world anyway? What precisely is it that God intends for us to be doing? What is our mission? What is our mandate? What does faithfulness in being the church look like? Many congregations would do well to spend some time wrestling seriously with questions like these.

The Church and Its Mission

At this point in my understanding of these issues the best answer I can give to the question of what it means to be the church is: The church is a community of people who are learning to live to the glory of God. Leith Anderson gives the best definition of the phrase "living to the glory of God" that I have heard. He explains that to live to the glory of God means to live in such a way that we enhance God's reputation in the world. As the church, our calling is to live in such a way that we represent God well, so that those who are estranged from God (whether through indifference, misinformation, or even hostility) will be attracted to and welcome God into their lives.

This is surely what is meant in the Epistle to the Ephesians when it says, in reference to the church, "we [are] for the praise of his glory" (1:12). Likewise, 1 Peter, again with reference to the church, says, "You are a chosen people, a royal priesthood, a holy nation, a people belonging to God, that you may declare the praises of him who called you out of darkness into his wonderful light" (2:9).

> *The church is a community of people who are learning to live to the glory of God.*

Behind all this, of course, is the marvelous story of the gospel of what God has done for us in Jesus Christ. This gospel (literally "good news") is the story of how God has acted in the life, death, and resurrection of Jesus Christ in order to rescue us from the power of evil and the penalty of sin and to reconcile us to himself (2 Cor. 5:17–6:2). It is the good news of how, in Jesus, God's kingdom has come among us. We are invited to turn from our preoccupations and priorities in order to enter the kingdom of God and begin learning how to live a new life with an entirely new focus and perspective (Mark 1:14-15).

But the gospel is not simply the story of what God has done in Jesus to fix what Satan has ruined and to reclaim what Satan has stolen. The gospel is an invitation. While the gospel proclaims important news, its proper form is always invitation. Jesus has made possible a new relationship with God and is inviting us to enter this relationship. Jesus has opened the doors of the kingdom of God; we are invited to enter the kingdom, now. The thing about invitations is that they require a response in order to be activated. The gospel invites us to be reconciled to God and to begin living the new life of the kingdom. This new life begins when we accept the invitation and turn to follow Jesus.[1]

The gospel forms the church and gives it its mandate. As the church, we have accepted this invitation and, having been reconciled to God through Jesus, are now learning to live the new life of the kingdom. As individuals and as congregations, we are called to enjoy a new relationship with God, to model the life of the kingdom in all that we do, and to work for the extension of God's kingdom throughout the whole world. This is what Jesus taught us to pray for in the petition, "Thy kingdom come. Thy will be done in earth, as it is in heaven" (Matt. 6:10 KJV).

All of this is summarized in this wonderful little phrase, "living to the glory of God." In a sense the church is Jesus' embassy, which he left on earth to represent him and carry out his mission. In the words of St. Paul, "We are . . . Christ's ambassadors (2 Cor. 5:20). Such a community does many things: It gathers for worship; it cares for its members; it works for justice and peace and reaches out with overtures of compassion and mercy; and it seeks to share the good news with everyone, to let them know of God's love and to invite them to accept the invitation of the gospel for themselves. But at the center, informing and connecting everything it does, this community understands that it exists to live for the glory of God.

My understanding of congregational leadership is that its primary responsibility is to envision what such a community might look like in this place at this time and then to nurture that community into being. Everything the congregation does, and everything it aspires to do and to become, should be tested against this goal.

The Gospel and Church Growth

The connection between this understanding of the church and the desire for growth is obvious. When we think of the church in this way, it is the most natural thing in the world to be concerned for our church's growth. The anticipation of growth is in the very nature of the gospel that forms the church. The gospel is, almost by definition, outwardly focused. It was Jesus, the one we follow and seek to please, who urged upon us the importance of sharing the gospel with everyone we can.[2] This is God's good news for the world; it is both the privilege and the responsibility of the church to share it.

> *While the gospel itself is not specifically about church growth, the ministry of sharing it inevitably leads to an invitation to come into the church.*

There are two basic models for sharing the good news. One is to do so in various ways outside the church, and then invite those who accept its invitation to come into the church and join the family; the other is to invite people to come into the life of the church and then explore the gospel and its invitation within the context of an accepting and supportive community. Either way, while the gospel itself is not specifically about church growth, the ministry of sharing it inevitably leads to an invitation to come into the church.

But, notice the difference between the motivation here and that of the reasons for seeking new members outlined earlier in this chapter. We are not talking about recruiting new workers or building a stronger financial base, or striving to authenticate our existence and look successful. Instead, we are seeking to help people connect with God and become followers of Jesus. We are acting out of a central motif of our God-given mission. Our primary goal is not to offer people the church but to offer them a new life in Christ—the life of the kingdom, which is really the goal of all of their striving and their heart's true home. The church is the community that is formed by kingdom people who together are celebrating this new life and learning how to live it.

It is interesting to note that as a by-product of this activity we will almost certainly end up with a stronger financial base and more people involved in ministry. In fact, we may even begin to look like we are thriving and give the impression that this church is an exciting place to be! But we hardly even notice this transi-

tion occurring. It is simply a result of remembering who we are
and what we are supposed to be about.

In my work with church leaders I often encourage them to give
up the burden of trying to save the church or even of helping it
to survive. Instead, I suggest that they take up the much more
invigorating work of developing a congregation that can pene-
trate their community with the gospel.

In so doing, there is a very good chance that in the process
they just might discover that their congregation is beginning to
thrive as well—but only as a by-product. After all, we are trying
to follow the one who taught that those who seek to save their
lives will lose them, while those who are willing to lose their lives
for the sake of the gospel will save them (Mark 8:35). This is as
true today as it was when Jesus first said it.

There's More to It Than Numbers

Whenever the matter of growth is raised in a congregation
there is sure to be someone who offers the opinion that there is a
lot more to church life than trying to grow. Some go so far as to
remark that the point is not about growth; it's about faithfulness.
Leaving aside the rather tempting question, Faithfulness to what?
I hope that what has been said so far is clear enough to avoid these
comments as objections to the point that I am making here. Of
course there is more to church life than trying to grow, but faithfulness does demand that we get out into the world with the wonderful invitation that God has asked us to extend in his name.

When asked, as I have been on occasion in my own congregation, How big is big enough for you? or, When do you think a
church has grown enough that it doesn't have to think about this
any more? the only answer I can possibly think of is, When we
are absolutely certain that we have reached everyone we can
reach; when we know for sure there is nobody else in this area
who still needs to know about the gospel and experience God's
love and grace, then I guess we can stop thinking about growth.

Until then we know without question what God wants us to be doing.

There is not only more to church life than numbers but also more to church growth than numbers. In his book *More Than Numbers*, Loren B. Mead shows that there are four distinct types of church growth.[3] The first is numerical growth, which is quite obvious and easy to assess. If you have more people this year than last year, that is numerical growth.

Maturational growth is another type, which refers to the growth of the people in the church in their life of faith toward spiritual maturity. And there is what Mead calls organic growth, which has to do with the quality of the congregation's corporate life as a community and all of the systems of communication and interaction within the congregation. Finally, incarnational growth has to do with the ministries of service and outreach offered by the congregation.

It is apparent that not all congregations have the same opportunities for numerical growth. There are a host of variables affecting this, and it might well be the case that for some congregations there is simply no hope for numerical growth at all. There are just too many things, including demographics and location, working against them. On the other hand, few congregations anywhere, regardless of size or location, cannot make some progress in the areas of maturational, organic, and incarnational growth.

My take on all of this is that if a congregation becomes intentional about maturational, organic, and incarnational growth, it has a much better chance of experiencing whatever opportunities there might be for numerical growth.

In other words, when a church addresses itself to the issues of helping its members grow in their faith, becoming a genuine community of love and support, and seeking to reach out and add value to the neighborhood in which it is set, it might discover that it is attracting new members as well.

When we think about numerical growth, we are looking for growth with integrity. If our focus becomes purely on numbers, we run the risk of forgetting who we are called to be and of resorting to various types of manipulation. On the other hand, if we decide prematurely that for us, numerical growth is impossible, we run the risk of being far less than we could be and of leaving untouched many whose lives could have been significantly influenced by our ministry. Finally, if we decide that in this congregation we are not really interested in sharing the gospel with others and inviting them in, then, quite simply, we are being unfaithful in this important part of our calling. A congregation that thinks this way is obviously neglecting the work of maturational growth because a community of people growing up in their faith would never decide that they were not interested in reaching others with the gospel that is transforming their own lives.

Three Focusing Questions

In addition to thinking through the foundational questions regarding the essence and mission of the church, there are three focusing questions that need to be faced by congregations pursuing growth with integrity.

The first is, In the lives of those we are seeking to reach, what do we want to see happen as a result of their coming within the sphere of influence of our ministry? Until we have a clear answer to this question, we really don't have much business trying to reach them. Given what has been said about the church as a community of people learning to live to the glory of God, the answer to this question has to be that we would like to see them become committed and enthusiastic followers of Jesus learning to live the new life of the kingdom.

Obviously the methods and details will vary from congregation to congregation but, given the purpsose of the church, any answer that falls short of this will be inadequate. The bottom line of all that we do is about seeing lives changed as we help people get connected with God and "seek first his kingdom and his righteousness" (Matt. 6:33). This is the overarching purpose of all that we do.

The second question is, What are we offering that from their point of view would make it worth their while to get involved with us? In *The Purpose-Driven Church*, Rick Warren comments

> *What do we want to see happen in their lives?*
> *What are we offering that from their point of view would make it worth their while?*
> *What price are we willing to pay?*

that "if you want to be able to catch fish you have to learn to think like a fish."[4] He is exactly right. As much as we might regret this fact, the truth is that the people we are seeking to reach with the gospel are not sitting around wondering if there is a church somewhere in the area that could use their help. We need to expect that their initial response to any overture to check out our church will be the silent (or perhaps not so silent) question, What's in this for me? Churches that attract significant numbers of unchurched people have learned to think like the unchurched and to approach things from their point of view.

The third question is, What price are we willing to pay in order to be able to reach them? There is always a price to be paid for growth. In the short term, it is always easier and cheaper to do nothing. New initiatives cost money, time, and energy. There are obstacles to be overcome; often the obstacles from within the congregation are at least as formidable as those encountered outside. The price is also paid in terms of change. A congregation serious about growth has to be willing to change. It won't always be obvious from the outset exactly what this change will look like, but as the process unfolds, change will be inevitable. And with the change there will probably come dissenting voices and even a sense of loss. This gives rise to the supplementary question, What will you allow to stop you? For many congregations the answer to this question is, The first dissenting comment. The correct answer to this question requires great wisdom and discernment. Fortunately, the scriptures promise these as well (James 1:5).

We now move on to consider the four categories of people every congregation can influence with the gospel and some of the things we need to keep in mind in order to do so.

CHAPTER TWO

THOSE IN THE PEWS

The first and most obvious group of people that any congregation can influence, of course, is those who are already in the pews, the current members, and this is where we should begin. If our goal is to be able to influence people with the gospel, it stands to reason that we should begin with those we already have. After all, if we can't influence them, we don't have much hope of being able to influence those we do not yet even know. But influence them how? To what end? For what purpose?

Understanding Discipleship

The first of the three focusing questions raised in the previous chapter was, In the lives of those we are seeking to reach, what do we want to see happen as a result of their coming within the sphere of influence of our ministry? On the basis of our discussion of the church and its purpose, we said that the answer to this question has to be about helping them become enthusiastic followers of Jesus who are learning to live the new life of God's kingdom. But, before we can desire this for those we would like to reach, we have to desire it for ourselves. After all, in seeking to reach outsiders we want to invite them to join us on the journey we have already begun. Our goal for our current members then is

> *As disciples of Jesus we are called to the lifelong adventure of learning to follow him closely and faithfully.*

to help them grow toward spiritual maturity so they can live more and more to the glory of God.

A good word for this process of growth and transformation is discipleship. In the Gospels, the earliest followers of Jesus were called disciples. In the so-called Great Commission recorded in Matthew 28:17-20, Jesus instructed these first disciples to "go and make disciples" (v. 19). When we become followers of Jesus, we become his disciples.

Disciples are learners. As disciples of Jesus we are called to the lifelong adventure of learning to follow him closely and faithfully. In learning to live to the glory of God, our desire is to become more like Jesus in thought, character, attitude, behavior, and purpose; to live lives that are pleasing to him in every way.

We want to be able to share more fully, more confidently, more joyfully, more enthusiastically, and more passionately in the mission of Jesus. We want to live in such a way that our words and deeds bear witness to the reality of God's reign.

As disciples of Jesus, our goal is to learn to live in such a way that our lives speak well of God and of his grace in Jesus Christ. We want to represent God well in all the places where we live our lives. We want our lives to attract people to God and to reflect God's desires for the world he created. This goal is what God calls us to as members of the church and is the point of all that we seek to do and desire to become.

It is important to note here that such lofty goals will never be completely realized, not by any congregation and not by any individual. Perfection is not for this earth; that's what heaven is for. The process of discipleship is undertaken by ordinary people from all conditions of life in whose hearts the invitation of the gospel has struck a responsive chord and who have turned to enter the new life of the kingdom. The church is a community of such people, every one of them in process, beginning from wherever they are and moving in a new direction with a new purpose.

Such people can only hope to reflect God's glory dimly and with a great deal of refraction, but the process of drawing closer to God and being transformed is what the adventure is all about, and also what brings glory to God.

> *We want our lives to attract people to God and to reflect God's desires for the world he created.*

The New Testament writers took it for granted that ongoing growth toward such spiritual maturity is the normal and natural dynamic of the Christian life. For those in their care they prayed for it, and they expected it. When they saw it, they thanked God; and when they did not see it, they were disturbed.

At one point, St. Paul scolds the Corinthians because they are growing too slowly, or perhaps, not at all. He tells them that rather than growing up in their faith they have remained infants. I want to be able to feed you solid food, he complains, but you can only handle milk (1 Cor. 3:1-3).

The author of the Epistle to the Hebrews has a similar complaint about those whom he is seeking to nurture, and he uses the same language. He tells them that solid food is for the mature, but they are not ready for it yet. He can only offer them milk because they are still infants. Although they should be capable of teaching others by now, they are still in need of elementary teaching themselves (Heb. 5:11-14).

On a more positive note, Paul informs the Philippians that he prays constantly for their continued growth toward spiritual maturity. "This is my prayer," he writes:

> that your love may abound more and more in knowledge and depth of insight, so that you may be able to discern what is best and may be pure and blameless until the day of Christ, filled with the fruit of righteousness that comes through Jesus Christ—to the glory and praise of God. (Phil. 1:9-11)

Making such disciples is the first and most important task of the church. In the final analysis, the ministry of the church and the work of God's kingdom can only be done by disciples, disciples who are growing up in their faith, developing a biblical worldview, understanding their faith and its implications more clearly, learning to make the connections between faith and everyday life, and developing the faith skills necessary to live the kingdom life. It follows then that everything else we do—from worship to witness to service—depends on this and cannot grow beyond it. What we do in this area determines what we become and what we accomplish in every other area of congregational life.

> *Making disciples is the first and most important task of the church.*
> *Everything else we do depends on this and cannot grow beyond it.*

It is worth pausing at this point to emphasize that even though this is a book about how congregations can grow, the true strength of a congregation is not measured by how many people show up week by week for worship or by the various programs and activities, nor is it measured by how many new people a congregation can attract and keep.

The true measure of congregational strength and vitality is how many people are being sent out—week by week—inspired, committed, and equipped to live to the glory of God and to do the work of the kingdom wherever their lives take them. Our ability to make disciples and send them into the world is the true measure of our effectiveness.

The good news is that there is no conflict here between quality and quantity. As Rick Warren reminds us so clearly, our goal is to make the best disciples we can and to make as many as we can.[1] As far as numerical growth is concerned, two further points need to be made.

The first is that we can't send them out equipped and able to live to God's glory if we haven't been able to bring them in to evangelize and disciple them.

The second is that a good discipleship training process will ultimately prove to be one of the most attractive things about your church that draws newcomers in.

The Problem

Sadly, somewhere along the line, many (perhaps most?) of our so-called mainline congregations have lost sight of their priority. Indeed, many people in our churches are not even aware that growth is part of the agenda. They understand that they are expected to show up, to pay up, and maybe even to shut up, but they have never been helped to understand that as Christians their primary calling is to grow up.

As a result many congregations are characterized by a deeply entrenched, thoroughgoing biblical illiteracy that reaches to even the most committed members. Many who have attended church faithfully for years, who have worked hard and given generously in support of their congregation, are unfamiliar with the key themes and characters of the Bible and do not know how to read the Bible for understanding and growth.

> *The failure to make disciple-making a priority is the basic cause of our current malaise and stagnation. It is the primary reason our local churches so often lack excitement and vitality.*

The same is true of prayer. Many lifelong Christians have never been helped by their church to develop a meaningful prayer life. They may or may not say a grace at mealtimes and throw up a prayer of desperation in difficult circumstances, but for many that is about as far as it goes. They do not really know how to pray for themselves or their families or their church; they do not know how to pray for or with their friends; and they would be extremely uncomfortable if ever asked to pray aloud in a Christian gathering. They simply would not be able to do it.

They also do not know how to witness to their faith with those who are unfamiliar with the gospel. For many years I have been leading conferences, workshops, and seminars on evangelism. Again and again the participants in these events, many of whom are lifelong churchgoers, have told me that one of the main reasons they do not share their faith with others is their lack of confidence that they understand it clearly enough to do so.

It is not that they wouldn't like to be able to do these things. The problem is they have never been taught because our churches have not made disciple-making a priority. Many people have related to me their experiences of trying to read the Bible or attempting to develop a daily pattern of prayer. Some have even shared their experiences of seeking to witness to their faith. Sometimes these experiences are hilariously funny, but the common denominator is that they have usually ended in discouragement and frustration.

There are various factors that have led to this situation. I believe the problem begins in our seminaries where candidates for congregational leadership and ordained ministry receive their training. As astonishing as this may seem to people unfamiliar with the situation, in most cases these candidates receive little or no training in this key area of helping people become mature disciples. Indeed, when I attended seminary, the subject was not even raised once in the course of a three-year degree program!

This is not the place for a detailed explanation; I will simply make the point here that this is a major challenge for our seminaries. The curriculum is already filled with interesting and important subjects. But somewhere, the candidates

> *We can never help people to grow up in their faith, to grow deeply into Christ, and to learn to follow him as committed disciples by protecting them from the call of the gospel.*

for ordained ministry and leadership need to be taught that making disciples is the primary work of the church and given practical, detailed help in how to do this work.

Candidates who trained in a system that has not identified disciple-making as the primary work and who serve their apprenticeship in congregations and with leaders for whom it is not a priority, will not make it a priority when charged with the leadership of their own congregation. With worship, pastoral care, community service, social justice, and many other things to take care of, disciple-making will simply slip off the board.

Besides, as clergy we are keenly aware that many of the people to whom we minister are extremely busy. They live hectic lives with huge responsibilities and pressures, and in seeking to be sympathetic to this, we are often loath to suggest that they should be putting more time into "church things." We are happy enough that they can even manage to show up for worship on Sunday morning.

The hesitation to suggest more church responsibility is understandable, but it is a temptation we must resist. We can never help people to grow up in their faith, to grow deeply into Christ, and to learn to follow him as committed disciples by protecting them from the call of the gospel. We have to help them understand that this is what the Christian life is all about and encourage them to prioritize their lives so that there is time for this. My experience is that we often underestimate what people are willing to do. They are willing to invest their time and energy in things that they know to be of value.

We seem to have developed a collective mentality that full-grown, mature disciples arrive on our church doorsteps ready-made, just looking for a place to serve, that somehow the work of discipleship has been done somewhere else. But where would that somewhere else be? Perhaps we assumed that because we live in a Christian culture we could take for granted that the work of discipleship was being done by the culture at large. But that assumption is a serious mistake. We do not live in a Christian culture. One of the most obvious facts of our time is that Christendom is dead.[2]

Mature disciples do not just appear, shaped and formed by our culture. No, disciples are made, slowly and painstakingly, most often from the raw material of self-centred, sinful, secular people.

> *Congregations that make discipleship a priority and become effective in helping their members grow are exciting places to be. They pulsate with excitement and anticipation.*

Given our culture how could it be otherwise? And, it is the work, the main work, of the church to make such disciples. There is no other place.

The failure to make disciple-making a priority is the basic cause of our current malaise and stagnation. It is the primary reason our local churches so often lack excitement and vitality. How could a congregation of people, even highly committed people, who do not know how to read the Bible, pray, or share their faith and who have only a vague and foggy understanding of what the church is all about in the first place, ever hope to influence this culture with the gospel or, for that matter, generate any sense of excitement about its mission among its members?

Indeed, if we are not able to encourage and help our current members to grow up in their faith, many of them will not understand why we want to reach others or what our goal is in trying to reach out. I have heard leading members in more than one congregation ask, Why all this fuss about trying to reach outsiders? They say it's a matter of personal taste and preference. Those who want to bring others in think primarily in terms of benefits to the church. "We need some new 'giving units,'" they say, or "we need some new workers to help us carry the load." Such attitudes betray an unfortunate misunderstanding of the gospel and the mission of the church. Sadly, such misunderstanding is all too common in many congregations.

I will say it again: It is growth in discipleship—developing a deeper understanding of the faith, nurturing a more intimate relationship with God, and learning to make the connections between faith and everyday life—that constitutes the real adventure and excitement of the Christian life.

Congregations that make growth a priority and become effective in helping their members grow are exciting places to be. They pulsate with excitement and anticipation. By the same token, the failure of many congregations to help their members grow becomes a major source of dissatisfaction and frustration that eventually expresses itself in unhealthy ways.

There can be no doubt that the key to congregational transformation lies in reclaiming this ministry as our number one priority. For the church that fails to do so, there is, to be quite blunt, no hope.

A Preliminary Curriculum for Growing Disciples

The Four Key Areas of Discipleship

If the goal of discipleship is learning to live to the glory of God, this quest will eventually touch every area of our lives. Nothing is left out. Discipleship is a process that is never finished. We can make great progress in the Christian life, but we can never say we have truly arrived. Discipleship is more a direction than a destination; it is a way of life. There is always more to learn.[3]

This means that it would be fruitless to attempt to list all the issues that could come into consideration over a lifetime of learning and growth. The list would be virtually endless. There are however four main subject areas into which these issues fall and which provide a good starting point for outlining a preliminary curriculum for growing disciples. These four areas indicate that balanced and healthy discipleship involves something for the head (there are things that we simply have to know), something for the heart (because discipleship is about a renewed relationship with God), and something for the hands (because the point of what we are learning is to change the way we live).

The Relationship

At its heart, Christianity is not so much about the rites and rituals of religion as it is about our relationship with God. When we were alienated from God by sin and were totally helpless, Jesus rescued us. Through him we have forgiveness of sins and a renewed relationship with God. This is what the Christian faith is all about. Knowing and living interactively with God is really the whole point of life.

Nurturing this relationship is an important part of growing up in our faith. We want it to be healthy, to grow deep and strong. We know from our human relationships that they require time and attention in order to grow. If they are neglected or taken for granted, they begin to deteriorate. The same is true of our relationship with God, which is why growing disciples develop the habit and discipline of setting aside time on a daily basis to nurture it.

We understand of course that we are always in God's presence. There is no place we can go where God is not with us. But that is quite a different thing from intentionally setting aside time to focus on God and nurture our relationship, which is accomplished through Bible reading, prayer, and worship. These are skills that we must learn. I suggest that people who are just beginning to develop this discipline start by setting aside ten minutes each day. The time can be increased as they become more comfortable with it. In this ten minutes we spend five minutes reading a biblical passage, one minute in reflection on what we have read, and four minutes in prayer. They will quickly discover that ten minutes is not nearly enough time and will want to increase it.

> *Discipleship involves something for the head, something for the hands, and something for the heart.*

Healthy relationships require times when we simply focus on each other and speak the language of love. In our relationship with God, it is what worship, praise, and thanksgiving are all about. Similarly, healthy relationships require a time when we can say we are sorry. There are things we have done that have affected our relationship in a negative way or things we could have done that would have been appreciated, but were neglected for whatever reason. For disciples, this is the language of confession. Our prayer time should include praise, thanksgiving, and confession as well as requests for help and guidance. I often tell people whom I am teaching to pray, "Everything you need to know about prayer you learned in kindergarten. Because it was there, or earlier, that you learned the importance of the words *thank you, sorry,* and *please.*" These are the words around which a healthy prayer life can be developed.

Information

Central to any serious discipleship process is continual development in our understanding of the basic content of the Christian faith. This content is the story that is told in the Bible and echoed in our creeds and eucharistic prayers. I referred earlier to the entrenched biblical illiteracy, which is characteristic of so many church members and congregations. This is a condition that needs to be acknowledged and addressed head-on.

To be biblically literate means to be familiar with the stories of scripture, the characters, the major themes, and the key words of the faith.

Beyond this, we need to understand the big story that the Bible tells, the story of creation, the fall, redemption, the mission of the church, and the ultimate consummation of history.

This is the story that tells us who we are and who our God is, where we have come from, what our lives are about, what our destiny is, and how we should live.

In the Bible we learn what the gospel is, what the church is, and what our mission is. It is this biblical story that provides the framework for our understanding of the world. We want so to immerse ourselves in this story that it becomes the framework through which we understand the world and the lens through which we see all of life. As we do, we will come to understand more deeply how the Bible challenges the basic assumptions and reigning values of our culture, and we will learn, slowly and painstakingly, what it means to be the people of God.

The Bible is the sourcebook of our faith and the indispensable guide of growing disciples. The Scriptures feed us, enlighten us, inspire us, and lead us. I believe that, for many of our congregations, our most immediate challenge in discipleship is getting our people into the Bible and getting the Bible into our people. The Bible needs to be taught, and people need to be taught how to read it, on their own and in small groups. Every congregation needs to be intentional, diligent, and creative in finding appropriate ways to do this.

Transformation

That God loves us and accepts each of us just as we are is an important part of the good news.

The corollary to this is equally important. We are loved so much that God has no intention of leaving us as God found us.

In almost every page of the New Testament Epistles, it is clear that a significant part of the growth of discipleship is transformation of character and behavior. One of Paul's consistent themes is that followers of Jesus are to put off the old self and put on the new. We are to lay aside the old life and grow up into the new life to which we have been called.

To the Galatians he writes, "the fruit of the Spirit is love, joy, peace, patience, kindness, goodness, faithfulness, gentleness and self-control" (Gal. 5:22). In a similar vein he exhorts the Colossians, "as God's chosen people, holy and dearly loved, clothe yourselves with compassion, kindness, humility, gentleness and patience" (Col. 3:12). In both of these passages he is drawing a contrast between the old nature and the new. He speaks of the two almost as though they are suits of clothes. Take off the old, he says, and put on the new.

In a wonderfully poetic passage Paul speaks of Christians coming to "reflect the Lord's glory, [and] being transformed into his likeness with ever-increasing glory" (2 Cor. 3:18). In his life Jesus exemplified the very essence of what it means to be fully human, and he is our model for life. We indicated earlier that our goal, as growing disciples, is to become more and more like him in thought, character, attitude, behavior, and purpose.

> *It is this transformation, more than anything else, which is the proof of God's work in our lives.*

For every one of us there is more than enough work here to last a lifetime. Success is not about becoming perfect; that's what heaven is for. Rather, it is about being changed over time and becoming more like Jesus than we are at present. It is this transformation, more than anything else, which is the proof of God's work in our lives. The adventure here is all in the process. Congregations of people who are being changed in this way truly bring glory to God. And they are magnetic; these are the types of congregations that people want to join.

Application

Application has to do with making the connections between faith and the everyday circumstances of our lives. The call to discipleship is not a call to turn our backs on the world. It is about a new way of being in the world as we learn to live the kingdom life. This call eventually embraces every area of life. It:

- influences our thinking and behavior in our homes, in our places of business and leisure, and in the church.
- involves new and deeper ways of understanding marriage, family, and sexuality.
- calls us to new ways of understanding work, career, success, and failure.
- calls us again and again to rethink the place of money in our lives and the ways we use our time.
- affects the way we treat others and challenges us to think about such issues as justice and our responsibility to care for God's creation.

Throughout a lifetime of discipleship we will learn more and more what it means to say no to ourselves and our own agendas in order to say yes to God and God's purposes for creation and history. We will learn to share more fully and appropriately in the mission and ministry of our congregations and to help them thrive. We will become more and more discerning of the signs of God's activity in the world around us and more adept at recognizing and resisting the false gods of our culture.

Our growing ability to make these connections will be the product of our increasing familiarity with scripture, the ongoing development of our prayer life, and the learning and encouragement we share with Christian friends engaged in the same adventure of discipleship.

Most of what we deal with as disciples will fall into one of these four main subject areas. Congregations seeking to grow healthy disciples will be thinking about them continually. We want to be able to provide appropriate help in each of these areas for people who are in the beginning, intermediate, and even advanced stages of discipleship.

The Three Dimensions of Discipleship

As we begin to unpack what it means to live as followers of Jesus we discover that there are three distinct, yet closely interrelated, dimensions to this life, each of which is informed by the four subject areas outlined previously. The three dimensions are the personal, the corporate, and the public. Most of us, for various, natural reasons, will probably feel more attracted to one or two of these dimensions and less attracted to the other one or two. Nevertheless, we must remember that balanced and healthy discipleship requires that we continue to grow in all three.

1. The personal dimension has to do with my understanding of myself as a child of God and my personal relationship with God, my growing understanding of the gospel and its implications, and the process of transformation through which I am becoming more like Jesus.

2. The corporate dimension has to do with understanding myself as a member of the people of God, the church. The Chris-

tian faith, from beginning to end, is a corporate faith. The gospel is certainly about the salvation of people as individuals, but it is about much more than that. It is about the new community that God is forming and calling to live to the praise of his glory. The call to follow Jesus is a call to join this community. Learning what it means to be a part of this community and to find our personal place of service within it is a foundational aspect of discipleship.

3. As surely as the gospel has both a personal and a corporate dimension, so it has a public dimension as well. God's purposes in the gospel do not end with the individual and his or her salvation, nor do they end with the church and its well-being. The ultimate concern of the gospel is the world and everything in it. The biblical vision is that God's reign will be acknowledged throughout the whole earth. As growing disciples we want to grow more and more in our ability to see the world from God's perspective and to understand more fully the height, the depth, and the breadth of the gospel and its implications for every area of our lives and for the whole world.[4]

Top Ten List of Topics for Discipleship

Having outlined briefly the four main areas and the three key dimensions of discipleship, I offer here my personal "top ten list" of topics for discipleship. This list is not exhaustive, of course, and each of these has been mentioned or alluded to above, but I offer them now in list form for the sake of clarity. Here then, are ten topics on which the leadership of a congregation should focus when seeking to help its members become well-grounded, balanced, mature disciples.

1. Teach them the gospel. Begin at the beginning, not in the middle. It is quite simply a fact that many of our members have only the sketchiest understanding of what the gospel is all about. We dare not assume that everyone currently in the pews understands it, much less that everyone has responded to God's offer of new life in Jesus Christ.

Teach them that the good news is about the kingdom of God and about reconciliation with God. The first of these deals with God's vision for creation and history. The second deals with the reality of sin and human alienation from God. Teach them that the gospel is an invitation for us to choose God's kingdom over against all the other voices and powers that call for our allegiance. Through Jesus Christ we are invited to be reconciled to God and to enter God's kingdom. Christian discipleship is about learning to live the life of God's kingdom.

2. Teach them what the church is. Help them understand the concept of "the people of God." Our mission in this world is to proclaim the kingdom of God in words and to model the kingdom of God in lifestyle and deeds, in contrast to the kingdoms and values of this world. We always need to keep in mind that our goal is to work for the extension of God's kingdom so that "[God's] will be done on earth as it is in heaven" (Matt. 6:10b). This is precisely what Jesus taught us to pray for, and most of us pray this in our services every week.

Many congregations would realize great benefits if they were to devote the next year in its entirety to teaching their current members what God calls the church to do and to be. Many of our most faithful members have had their understanding of the church shaped by the expectations and assumptions of a "Christendom" worldview. Because they assume (incorrectly) that we live in a Christian society, they have a rather truncated understanding of the church's mission in our contemporary "post-Christendom" situation. This desperately needs to be corrected if we are to be effective in the current cultural context.

3. Teach them how to read the Bible in a responsible and intelligent way. Many of them have no idea how to even begin reading the Bible. Explain to them the two major divisions—the Old and New Testaments—and that the Bible is not one book, but rather a library of books, written and compiled over a number of centuries, through many different cultural contexts.

Help them understand the "big picture" by giving them an overview of the biblical story, teaching them about the various types of literature the Bible contains, and showing them where the various books fit into biblical history. Help them with the "smaller picture" by teaching them how to read for personal learning and growth and by helping them develop a pattern of daily reading. Help them, too, to engage in biblical reflection in small group situations, sharing their insights and questions and listening for God's voice as it emerges through the group.

4. Teach them how to pray in an informed and disciplined way. As noted earlier, many of our current members have absolutely no confidence in their ability to pray. (They have always thought this was something the clergy did for them.) Teach them about various approaches to prayer and the various types of prayer. Teach them how to pray for themselves, for their families and friends, for the church, and for the world. Scripture provides many examples of such prayers.

Teach them the importance of listening in prayer, as well as of speaking. Give them a formula for spending ten minutes each day with God in Bible reading and prayer, encouraging them to increase this time daily as they develop the habit of daily devotions. Give them a sample outline of what 30 minutes might look like and then of what is involved in spending one hour reading scripture, reflecting, and praying.

5. Teach them the ministry of reconciliation. Help them to understand that as followers of Jesus they are called to share with God in the important work of reconciling the world to God and extending God's kingdom. Teach them that God has given them unique and special gifts to equip them for their particular place in this work. Help them to understand the concept of "the body of Christ" in which each of us have different functions to which we must attend if the body is to function in a healthy way. As they begin to discover their own gifts for ministry, help them find appropriate opportunities to exercise them.

6. Teach them about the place of worship in the life of the Christian community and in the lives of growing disciples. Misunderstandings about the nature and purpose of worship plague our church and contribute to the kind of vitriolic arguments and debates that debilitate us with regard to practical, effective mission and outreach. Teach them that worship is the

language of love, that it has far more to do with astonishment at the love and grace of God and with offering ourselves to live the life of God's kingdom and to work for its extension than it does with loyalty to inherited forms and traditions.

7. Teach them solid principles of financial stewardship. The driving force behind good financial stewardship is not, How much money does my church need? but rather, How much do I need to give in order to be set free from the lies I have learned from our secular culture about the importance of money?

Teach them the importance of proportional giving and of giving "off the top" rather than from what is left over when everything else has been looked after. Teach them that the disciple's motivation for giving is gratitude rather than duty, and that, How much *can* I give? is a much better question than, How much *must* I give? Teach them that developing a proper attitude toward money could well be their biggest challenge and the single most important factor in determining their potential for continued spiritual growth.

8. Teach them to develop a Christian mind. Teach them that mature faith is a filter through which every area of life is passed and evaluated rather than a set of religious beliefs that are simply added to an essentially secular worldview. Hold out the challenge of developing a Christian mind, which will help them in their daily decisions and responsibilities to discern what is best from a kingdom perspective. Teach them that the Christian mind is shaped gradually through constant attention to corporate worship and daily time in scripture reading, prayer, and discipleship conversations with other growing Christians.

9. Teach them the importance of bearing witness to their faith in the course of their daily lives, within their natural spheres of influence. Teach them how to do so in a straightforward, inoffensive manner as opportunities arise. Teach them that evangelism is important because we are learning to follow the greatest evangelist of all, Jesus himself. Teach them that evangelism is important because people matter to God.

10. Teach them about the presence and work of the Holy Spirit in the lives of growing disciples, empowering them for the life of

the kingdom, and transforming their character and nature to become more like Christ. Help them to develop a healthy and balanced understanding of the work of the Holy Spirit and to maintain a healthy balance between personal piety and publicly living the life of the kingdom.

Think *Process* Before *Program*

As we well know, congregations differ widely in size, style, leadership gifts, experience, education, and a host of other variables. Every congregation has its own personality, history, and tone. This makes it impossible to develop a neatly packaged, comprehensive and generic program of discipleship that would suit every congregation. For this reason it is better to think *process* before thinking *program* in this area. One size, style, or method definitely does not fit all.

In some congregations it might be appropriate to put on full-scale courses and conferences; other congregations will find it better to opt for occasional seminars, workshops, and weekend retreats; some congregations will do this training in small groups, or through spiritual mentors, while still others might find that personal conversations with various people and books and tapes work best for them.

On the other hand, these congregational variables do not change the basic issues in which disciples need training and instruction. What they do affect is the way in which this training and instruction is given. My advice is to take these ingredients and play around with them—thinking, praying, brainstorming, experimenting—as you seek to develop a process of disciple-making that fits your unique situation. Remember, there is no particular right way to do this; the question is, What is most appropriate and effective for you?

No matter what you eventually come up with (and it should never be static; keep it growing; keep finding ways to do it better; keep adding new issues and items), the single most important aspect of this whole process is creating within the congregation

the expectation of growth and nurturing a congregational climate within which growth can occur. We need to make this
expectation a core value of our congregations.

In my consulting work I have had many congregational leaders tell me that the people in their congregations simply are not
interested in growth. "We can't get them to come out" is the
common lament. I have a hard time believing that this is true. In
most cases, I suspect the necessary groundwork of creating the
expectation of growth as the normal condition of the Christian
life and nurturing a climate of growth has not been done. There
are no shortcuts here. But, once people understand that the
adventure of Christian living lies in continual growth and that
their congregation is devoted to helping them in this, they will
be there.

The key is in presenting this in such a way that people can
begin to sense the benefits of growth and the difference it will
make in their lives. We need to cast such a compelling vision of
who they can become in Christ that they can't wait to get at it.
Unfortunately, Christian commitment is often presented in such
sterile terms that people's initial response is, "How cheaply can I
get the benefits of
Christianity, and how
long can I defer the pay-
ments?" What we want to
do is present such a com-
pelling vision of who they
can become, along with
the assurance that we
have a process for helping
them get there, that their
immediate response is,
"How quickly can I get
started?" We want to help
them see that this growth
and this relationship with Jesus is what they have been searching
for for a long time, but perhaps they haven't had the language to
express it!

> *The single most
> important aspect of this
> whole process is creating
> within the congregation
> the expectation of
> growth and nurturing a
> congregational climate
> within which growth
> can occur.*

Looking Outward

When a significant number of our members are beginning to understand what Christian growth is about and are entering into the process of discipleship, we are ready to begin looking outward and thinking about how we can influence others. Now they can begin to understand why it is important to do so. They realize that the calling of the church in mission is not simply to attract new members in order to perpetuate itself, but rather to share the good news with people who need to know God. They are able to see that this evangelistic outreach is for the sake of people who matter to God, not for the sake of the church.

As they continue to grow and to understand the importance of this imperative, they will be more and more willing to evaluate everything the church does from the perspective of how it helps or hinders this mission and will be prepared to make the necessary changes and suffer the various inconveniences and sacrifices involved in embracing this mission with passion and enthusiasm.

Only growing disciples who are excited by the work of God in their lives and by the prospects of reaching others with the good news are able and willing to face these questions and follow their lead. Here is the "secret" of church growth: If you want your church to grow, help your members to grow. More often than not, growing churches are the by-product of growing people.

With this in place, we move on now to consider the second category of people your congregation can influence.

THOSE WHO WALK IN

The second group of people most congregations can influence is those who walk in. These are the people who simply show up as visitors on a Sunday morning to join the regular congregation in worship. Most frequently these visitors are not acquainted with any of the regular members. All on their own they have sought out this congregation, made the effort to find out what time the service begins, and have shown up at the door as complete strangers. This happens every Sunday morning all across the country in congregations of all shapes and sizes.

Obviously, all visitors are not created alike. They do not all fit one particular profile, and they are not all prospects for membership in your congregation. Some of them are just passing through, perhaps from out of town, seeking a place to worship on this particular morning. Others are members of another congregation in the area, looking for a break in their regular routine this morning or perhaps, for various reasons, looking for a new congregation to join.

In this case, time alone will tell whether such a change would be good for them and for you. The bottom line, though, is that no congregation can ever experience healthy, long-term growth simply by attracting members from other congregations. The goal of evangelism and church growth is to reach those who are out-side the faith and outside the church. There is a world of differ-ence between bringing unchurched nonbelievers to a vital faith in Christ and moving church members around from congregation to congregation. One is primary growth, the other secondary. Healthy congregations experience both, but their main goal is always primary growth.

Some of your walk-in visitors will have just moved into your neighborhood and will be seeking a new church in which to put down their roots. These people are good prospects for member-ship in your congregation. They will need some time to take the measure of your congregation and determine whether or not it is a good fit for them, but they might well turn out to bring signifi-cant gifts for ministry that will help your congregation to thrive.

Still others are coming to church for the first time in many years, in some cases perhaps, for the first time in their lives! With this group you can be fairly certain that something significant is going on in their lives. In our prevailing cultural climate it is highly unlikely that people who have not attended church for many years, or perhaps not at all, would suddenly show up on a Sunday morning out of idle interest. It might happen, but not too often. People are too busy, and they have too many options for how to spend their discretionary time. No, when such people make the effort to come onto our territory as strangers, you should take it for granted that something significant is going on in their lives.

The simple act of showing up on Sunday is often the most important signal a person can give a church that something important is going on in their lives and they are open for spiritual discovery and change. George Hunter, having conducted thor-ough research into why unchurched people suddenly show up in church, observes,

> I have learned, through interview research, that most pre-Christian visitors to a church feel anxious and vulnerable as they visit "foreign turf" but, often, something is going on in their life that they think a church might help with. Most

church leaders, however, have never taken seriously the non-verbal communication that a visiting seeker is sending out. Their visit is the most misperceived signal in local churches today, and the church's most neglected opportunity.[1]

They probably won't tell you what it is that first morning (indeed, they might not even know themselves what it is that motivated them to come), but if you can manage to keep them coming back for long enough, eventually you will hear an interesting story. I can almost guarantee it. I still get excited when these newcomers show up in my congregation on a Sunday morning, because long experience has taught me that there is the possibility here of becoming involved in some really exciting growth and change in their lives in the next little while.

Keeping in mind the mission of the church, our primary goal for this second group—those who walk in—is to disciple them toward Christian maturity, just as we seek to do with our current members. But before we are able to do this we must be able to make them feel at home and comfortable among us. They must know that they are welcome and that we would be happy to have them join with us in our adventure of faith. The basic issue here is whether or not your visitors get the sense that this congregation is expecting company, ready for company, and really wants company. People will not usually stay long in a place where they do not feel welcome or where they do not feel comfortable.

Our strategy for these people then is (1) welcome and assimilate them into the life of our congregation, and (2) disciple them to spiritual maturity as committed followers of Jesus.

Think Friendly

Part one of this strategy, welcoming and assimilating, begins with simple old-fashioned friendliness. In a car dealership, I once saw a plaque on the wall of a salesman's office that said "Be A Shopper Stopper." That is the congregational perspective that we want to develop toward our visitors. We want to be able to connect with them in such a way that they will want to return again and again, and eventually become a part of our congregation. It is easy to be a Teflon congregation that visitors just slide through; that doesn't take any effort at all. But we want to become Velcro congregations that help visitors stick. This is the only way that we will be able to influence them toward Christ and help them to grow. The first key to bringing them back is a warm and friendly welcome when they come.

It is important then to deliberately cultivate and nurture a congregational atmosphere of friendliness toward visitors. This should be a core value in every congregation. This seems obvious but it is sometimes more difficult than it sounds. Part of the problem is that most (perhaps all) congregations truly believe that they are genuinely friendly. They would be mortified to think that perhaps they are not. In countless workshops on congregational development I have asked people to list their congregation's greatest strengths; in almost every instance "friendliness" ranks in the top three.

> *The reason most church members think their congregation is friendly is because they have good friends there, and when they are at church they are spending time with their friends.*

The important question that needs to be asked in these situations is, Who told you that you are friendly? Self-commendation in this matter should be regarded as highly suspect. The reason most congregations believe they are friendly is because when the regular members go to church, they meet their friends there. So, of course they believe they are part of a friendly church.

But, while all the regular members are having a great time chatting and laughing with their friends, visitors and strangers might be forming an entirely different opinion as they look on. They might well be thinking, "this place is a closed shop; they haven't even noticed I am here; they are all so busy with each other they don't have any time for newcomers." It's not that the regular members are trying to be unfriendly. It's just that they have been preoccupied in catching up with their friends whom they haven't seen all week. The stories of people going to churches and leaving feeling they have hardly been noticed are legion. Meanwhile, the members go home confirmed in their belief that theirs is truly a friendly church.

But, growing Christians are coming to understand the importance of being able to connect with others in order to influence them toward Christ. As they see people coming to Christ, they pray that their congregation will be able to help many to do so. They both want and expect visitors to join them for worship on Sunday mornings, and they are prepared to go out of their way to make sure they feel welcomed. They realize that these visitors might well be signaling, just by showing up, that they are wide open to the gospel. As Howard Hanchey has reminded us in his wonderful book on evangelism and church growth, there are so many options otherwise available to people on Sunday mornings that those who just walk in should be regarded as the personal guests of Jesus.[2] It is Jesus who has motivated them to come, and as such they are deserving of special attention.

Putting Ourselves in Their Place

Congregational friendliness begins by putting ourselves in the place of the visitor and seeking to understand something of what they might be feeling as they come to join us in worship for the first time. It is difficult for us to imagine, as we enter our familiar sanctuary to worship with our friends, that anyone could possibly find this a stressful situation. How could they? What could

> *Congregational friendliness begins by putting ourselves in the place of the visitor and seeking to understand something of what they might be feeling as they come to join us in worship for the first time.*

be stressful in this nice place? But as the visitors approach the church and find their way in for the first time chances are strong that stress and anxiety are precisely what they are feeling.

They are coming into a new place, filled with strangers who all seem to know each other. Perhaps they are unsure of what kind of service and what kind of reception awaits them. Will they be noticed? Will they be welcomed? Will they know what to do? Will they fit in? Is there any chance that they might be embarrassed in some way? In addition, they might well be going through a stressful period in their lives; maybe that is why they are here today. What if they are coming here today feeling that this church is their last hope? With all this on their minds, I truly believe that most visitors are demonstrating tremendous courage simply by showing up! They deserve to be welcomed warmly and treated with dignity and respect.

Welcoming our visitors properly is a delicate art. We need to pay attention to them and let them know that they are noticed and welcome. We need to be friendly toward them and help them feel at ease, but at the same time, we must avoid embarrassing them or smothering them. We need to give them space to size us up while getting the message across that we are delighted they are here. All of this is far too important to be left to chance on the assumption that we are a friendly congregation and things will just take care of themselves.

How welcoming is done will obviously vary from congregation to congregation and will certainly depend in some measure on the size and location of the congregation. Some congregations might well have scores of visitors on any given Sunday; for others, everyone in the congregation knows immediately when there is a newcomer on the premises. Likewise some congregations are set in neighborhoods where most people hardly know even their next-door neighbors, while others are in settings where everyone knows everyone else and has a detailed sense of each family's history as well. (In this case, a proper welcome can be much more challenging than where people hardly know each other.)

The challenge for every congregation is to develop a form and a style of welcome that is appropriate for its circumstances. What follows are a few things that should be kept in mind as this process is thought through. Not all of them will apply in every situation, and I am sure that every congregation will think of many more issues that are not included here. Nevertheless, this can help to prime the pump for us as we think about what is most appropriate for us.

Some Practical Considerations

Arriving

A genuinely welcoming congregation understands that friendliness begins outside the building. Will visitors know where to park? Are there parking spots reserved for visitors? Are they the best spots? (Why is the spot closest to the door usually marked "Reserved For Clergy"? What is that about? I was once invited to a church to lead a workshop on the topic of congregational friendliness. The first thing I saw when I entered the parking lot was a sign at the best spot that said, "Reserved For Clergy; All others will be towed." I knew precisely where to begin the workshop.) Will others in the parking lot speak to them as they get out of their car and walk toward the church, or will they feel like they are being stared at? Is the property well signed, inside and out? Is it clear which entrance is the one to use?

Is there a glass door that they can see through before they enter, or will they have to open a huge solid door, not knowing what to expect on the other side until they have made their entrance? Let's take a cue here from retail business establishments that seek to put people at ease as they approach and enter their premises. Restaurants, banks, and stores all know the value of plenty of glass. People like to know what they are walking into. It reduces their stress. The establishments in my area that have big solid doors and leaded windows are intentionally sending the message that they are private and exclusive; visitors are not wanted; this place is for members only. Those who are seeking to attract people use lots of glass!

Will they know where the washrooms are, where the nursery is, what the arrangements are for the children's program? These are some of the basic questions that will be on their minds.

Congregations interested in growth take the guesswork out of all this for their visitors by putting themselves in their shoes long before they ever show up. They think these things through carefully and leave nothing to chance. This is simply a way of showing respect for these guests of Jesus.

Train your ushers and greeters to be on the lookout for these people and to be aware of the anxiety they are probably feeling. Teach them to anticipate visitors' questions and be ready to volunteer helpful information. Remind them that your church only gets one chance to make a first impression with these visitors, and they will be in the very front line of contact. Most visitors have made a preliminary judgment within a few minutes of entering the building as to whether they will be back again. These first few minutes are crucial. Respect, dignity, grace, and help are the important words here.

Impress upon your greeters the importance of making eye contact with people when welcoming them. On more than one occasion I have had the experience of going into a church as a stranger and being handed a service leaflet by a greeter who was busily engaged in conversation with a friend and didn't even bother to look at me. It has happened in my own church! One Sunday morning I walked in the front door just before the service was to begin and the greeter, joking with a friend, handed me a leaflet while his head was turned away from me. He didn't even look at me! So I tapped him on the shoulder and said, "Remember, make eye contact with everyone!" He was quite astonished to see that it was his minister speaking, but I think he took the message to heart.

But, friendliness does not mean being overbearing or assuming too much. A woman once told me of her experience of showing up as a stranger at a church and on her way in being handed a box of offering envelopes by an overly zealous elder. Another man related the experience of going to a church for the first time and being asked if he would like to help take up the offering next week. This is not good form.

The Worship Service

Will the regular members coming into the worship area have been thoughtful enough to leave some seats empty near the back so that newcomers can slip in as unobtrusively as possible? Or, will they have to walk up the aisle, in full view of everyone, and sit at the front? Remember, because they don't know anyone there, chances are they are not going to show up very early; they will probably time it to arrive just a minute or two before the service begins. If they have to sit near the front, they will probably feel vulnerable and conspicuous, sensing that the whole congregation is watching them. Remember that they are probably planning on taking their cues on how to participate in the service from the rest of the congregation. This will be difficult to do if most of the congregation is seated behind them. Visitor-friendly congregations help their guests slip in inconspicuously.

> *The leaflet will send out a lot of silent signals to visitors about your congregation's attitude to newcomers.*

As for the service itself, will it be visitor-friendly? Perhaps a few words at the beginning of the service, addressed particularly to visitors and assuring them that they are welcome, would help. In most cases it is best not to draw undue attention to them by asking them to introduce themselves in the service, or to wear special name tags, or by pinning flowers on them, or anything else that makes them stand out. A very few might possibly enjoy this; most won't.

Were visitors kept in mind when the service leaflet was being prepared? The leaflet will send out a lot of silent signals to visitors about your congregation's attitude to newcomers. Are there terms in it that they might not understand? If so, how can this be remedied so they don't feel excluded? Notices like "The Overcomers group meets on Tuesday night at Don and Shirley's" send a clear signal that this congregation is insensitive toward visitors. To the newcomer, this sounds very much like a place for those who are in the know.

It is immensely helpful if those who are leading the service explain what is happening as the service proceeds. They should also give clear directions as to what is expected by way of participation. Is everyone to join in on this response? Should we stand, remain seated, or kneel? Which book are we using? Where should we look for the words of this song? What is the historical setting and issue involved in the Bible reading? Did this event take place before, during, or after the time of Jesus?

In liturgical churches, I have often met the objection that such explanations interrupt the flow of the liturgy. Of course they do. But if the choice is between a smooth-flowing liturgy and treating newcomers with respect so that we might be able to influence their spiritual growth, and perhaps even their conversion, the choice is not even an issue for me.

In the previous chapter we spoke of entrenched biblical illiteracy among church members. How much more is this the case among visitors, some of whom have not been in church for many years? They are probably keenly aware of their lack of familiarity with the Bible and the vocabulary of faith. They are likely feeling quite uneasy about it, wondering whether or not it will be exposed in some way. Friendliness here involves helping them to relax and feel at ease.

After the Service

Following the service it helps to have the congregation practice the "ten foot rule." This rule simply states that I will greet everyone within ten feet of me, whether I know them or not. A simple greeting is sufficient: "Hi, my name is Harold. I don't think I've had the pleasure of meeting you before." This is usually enough to begin a short conversation.

Once it is established that this person is a newcomer, the conversation could include an invitation to come with you to coffee hour, the offer to introduce them to some of the others there, the offer to help with any questions they might have about the congregation or the premises, and a sincere expression that you hope they have enjoyed their visit and that they will come again. None of this is difficult. Anyone can do it. It is all a question of attitude and sensitivity.

Following Up

Without a warm welcome it is unlikely that any but the most tenacious of newcomers will return. But, there is a world of difference between being friendly to visitors and having in place a process to help assimilate them into the life of your congregation. The two go hand in hand, but they are quite distinct.

Remember that there is a qualitative difference between the first visit and the second. On the first visit, the newcomer is checking your congregation out. The next few visits indicate that they have been favorably impressed and are taking you seriously. But a second or third visit does not mean they have been assimilated. Very soon you will have to offer them more than a friendly greeting in order to keep them coming back.

Congregational variables such as size and location will obviously have a major influence on the manner in which any congregation seeks to assimilate its newcomers. As in so many other issues in congregational life, what is appropriate and effective in one situation is entirely inappropriate and ineffective in another. This is not a matter of right and wrong. Here are a few suggestions to keep in mind as you think through what is most appropriate for you.

Get Their Names

Before you can do anything else in welcoming and assimilating your newcomers, you have to know who they are. You will need to find an appropriate way of getting at least their name, address, and phone number. It is probably best to assume that not all of your visitors will feel comfortable in giving you such personal information on their first visit. It is good to have some mechanism such as a newcomer's form readily available should they desire to do so, but understand that there might be some reluctance to do so early on.

Never force this issue. It is good practice to indicate that you understand that they may feel uncomfortable filling out this form but that you would encourage them to do so when they do feel comfortable. Assure them that this information will only be used to enable you to contact them and to send them some information about your church, to help them decide whether this might be a good church for them. In speaking to visitors on Sunday mornings I usually say something like this:

> "There is a Newcomer's Form in the leaflet you received on the way in this morning. If you feel comfortable in filling that in, with your name, phone number, and address, we would love for you to do so. That information will not be used for any other purpose than to help us make an initial contact with you this week, in order to get you some information about this church and to see how we might be of help to you. If you would rather wait a bit before filling it out we understand. But please do so whenever you feel ready. In the meantime we hope that you enjoy your contact with this congregation and that you will consider getting to know us better and helping us to get to know you."

We find that most people fill the form out within the first two or three visits. Some take much longer. Some never do. Until they do, we let them keep their distance. Once they fill out the form, we feel comfortable in taking some initiative toward them. Filling out the form is their signal that they are ready to hear from us.

Pay Them a Visit

In most cases, once they have trusted you with their name, address, and telephone number, newcomers should receive a personal visit from an appropriate representative of the congregation. The purpose of this visit is to pay them some personal attention in order to let them know that they are truly welcome in your congregation and to answer any questions they may have. This visit is an important step in the process of helping them ease their way in. It is important to remember that this visit is for their sake. It should not normally be used to recruit them for service in the church, nor to inquire too deeply into their spiritual history or faith convictions. Getting too personal at this early stage might well scare them off.

The visit should not be too long; they are not expecting you to spend the evening with them! Remember to respect their time. In some communities it might be appropriate simply to show up at their home for a brief visit without first making arrangements; in other communities this would be a big mistake. Think this through carefully. In our congregation we always arrange this visit by telephone; some people welcome the visit, others make it quite clear that they do not want one.

Have a Newcomers' Event

In congregations that attract a lot of visitors and newcomers it might be appropriate to have a special event on a regular basis to which all newcomers are invited to meet one another and some of the key leaders in the church. This event might take the form of a coffee and dessert evening or a Sunday luncheon. This is an ideal time to talk with them about the goals and purposes of the church and for them to get to know one another. It is also a good time to talk with them about the various groups, programs, and activities of the church so they get a sense of the bigger picture and hear of some things that might be of special interest to them. In our congregation we have a quarterly Newcomers' Dessert and Coffee Evening, where we try to give them an overview of what is going on in the church. This event goes a long way toward reassuring our newcomers that they are important to us and that we take them seriously.

Finding the Way In

In attempting to help your newcomers find an appropriate track into the life of your congregation, it is probably helpful to focus on three main areas of congregational life:

- help them make friends
- offer pastoral care
- help them develop faith

Help Them Make Friends

One of the most important factors in assimilating newcomers is helping them to make friends. Common sense tells us that those who make friends in a congregation are far more likely to stay than those who don't. The truth here is that people come to a church for many reasons but usually stay because they make good friends. Perhaps more than any other single issue, the ability to make friends in the congregation will determine whether they stay or move on.

Following the initial home visit, the representative should be actively thinking about members of the congregation whom they might enjoy getting to know. So should everyone else they meet! Introducing newcomers to others in the congregation who seem to have various things in common with them should become second nature for all of us. This is one of the most simple and effective ways of assimilating newcomers into your church.

A healthy assimilation process, then, will provide plenty of opportunities for helping people get to know one another on a social basis so that friendships can begin to develop. Congregational life must be more than a series of parties but rather a good variety of social events, carefully planned to include good food and lots of opportunity for conversation. This will provide newcomers with an enjoyable and nonthreatening way to get to know others and begin to feel at home.

There might even be special events arranged for no other purpose than to help a new person or family meet particular members of the congregation who live on their street, live in their neighborhood, or have other interests in common. Maybe someone would host

> *Common sense tells us that those who make friends in a congregation are far more likely to stay than those who don't.*

a barbecue or dessert party and invite the newcomers, saying simply, "We would love to have you over to meet some of the other people in the church who live around here and to help us all get to know each other a bit better." Simple friendliness goes a long way! There is no substitute for it.

Offer Pastoral Care

Your newcomers will also want to know what forms of pastoral care you are able to provide. Remember that some of them may have come hoping that this church will be able to help them with some difficult issue.

Don't assume that they will know automatically how to access this care, but do assume that they might well feel somewhat embarrassed or uneasy about their need.

Find various gentle ways to let your newcomers know that many people first come to a church because they are looking for help with some personal need and that such inquiries are welcome. Explain that helping people get their lives together and back on the road to wholeness is a major issue in the Christian faith and that this church loves to help people whenever it can. Reassure everyone that this is a normal and important aspect of congregational life.

Let people know how pastoral care is provided, what resources are available, and how this care may be accessed. The assurance of confidentiality in this will be particularly important to people who are feeling fragile and vulnerable. The more you are able to do in this area, the greater your power to attract and assimilate newcomers will be.[3]

Help Them Develop Faith

It is important to be clear with newcomers from the very beginning about the purpose of your church. Let them know what you are about and what you are seeking to accomplish. Do you have a mission statement? Explain it to them. Do you have some core values? Share them. Do you have some specific goals and objectives you are seeking to accomplish in the next year or two? Tell them what they are and why they are important.

> *It is important to be clear with newcomers from the very beginning about the purpose of your church.*

More important, let them know what you want to see happen in the lives of the people who share in the life of your congregation. Tell them that you are in the business of helping people live to the glory of God, serving him joyfully and confidently in the various places and circumstances in which they live their lives.

Let them know that helping people in this way is what everything in this congregation is geared toward; this is what you are all about.

Tell them that you would love for them to join you in the great adventure of Christian living and that your congregation can help and encourage them in their ongoing faith development and spiritual growth. Tell them plainly and simply that you are convinced that helping people live to the glory of God is the very best thing the church can do for them or for anyone in this congregation; ultimately it is all we have to offer that is of lasting value. In my own congregation, I have been saying these things to newcomers for years, and I have never known anyone to take offense. More often than not, I am aware that these words are falling like refreshing rain upon parched ground; they are words of vision and of hope. People want to be part of a church that is seeking to help them with the deepest questions and issues of life.

I am always surprised to discover that congregations are timid about mentioning this to newcomers. We are willing to talk about all kinds of other things with them but feel uneasy about God talk. It is almost as if we think they wouldn't understand that we are about helping people connect with God. But this is why they have come. They are well aware that the church is about helping people with issues of faith and life. Our desire to talk with them about spiritual growth and faith development will not come as a surprise to them. They fully expect it and, in most cases, will be relieved to know that they have come to a church that is quite clear about this. Churches that are reluctant to speak openly about God and faith in Jesus Christ just puzzle people.

It goes without saying that all of this must be done in a spirit of support and encouragement, not of judgment and condemnation. Again, to use a personal example, in our congregation we explain to everyone that we are trying to be "fuzzy at the edges and solid at the center." By this we mean that we have no entrance requirements; absolutely everyone is welcome in this place. There is nothing you could have done that would make you unwelcome here or disqualify you for participation in the life of this congregation.

But that does not mean that we have no convictions or standards of belief and behavior. It simply means that we welcome everyone to come just as they are and to begin where they are. But we also make clear that as they allow us to guide them, at their pace, to the center of what we are all about, they will discover a rock-solid foundation

> *Congregations that are willing to begin with people where they are and to help them grow from there will be extremely attractive to newcomers.*

of belief and conviction. We explain that, as they discover more about who Jesus is and the life of discipleship to which he invites them, they will become aware of all kinds of connections with their lives that will have to be thought through. But our commitment is to begin with everyone just as they are and help engage them in this journey of faith.

Help Them Start at the Beginning

We have seen that it is a mistake to assume that our newcomers normally arrive with a well-developed faith, looking for an opportunity to use their spiritual gifts to enhance the ministry of our church. In today's culture, it is better to assume that, in most cases, they will have, at best, a sketchy and possibly misinformed understanding of what the Christian faith is all about, and the kind of life to which it calls them. But they are on a spiritual quest. Congregations that are willing to begin with people where they are and to help them grow from there will be extremely attractive to newcomers. There is nothing quite like a clear sense of purpose and direction, and the offer of practical help.

Remember that our goal is not simply to assimilate them for the sake of increasing the size of our congregation. Our ultimate goal is to disciple them toward spiritual maturity as committed followers of Jesus, so that they may be able to live to the glory of God. Helping them with the basics is not only an important step in their assimilation into the church but also the first step in the process of discipleship discussed in the previous chapter. Wise congregations think this through very carefully and work hard at finding appropriate ways to help newcomers with the basics. Don't make the mistake of assuming too much and starting in the middle with them. This will only confuse them. Find a way to start at the beginning.

Many congregations are finding the Alpha program to be a tremendous help. For many years in our congregation a four-week course, which we developed with the title "Christian Basics" and more recently renamed "Christianity 101," has been used with great results. The course consists of four presentations (one each week) on the following topics: "There is something wrong with the world"; "What, if anything, is God doing about this?" "How am I supposed to respond to this?" and "Where do I go from here?" This outline allows us to present the gospel simply and clearly, beginning from their own experience of living in a broken world and trying to make sense of it.

Each session consists of "warm up" conversations, a chance for the participants to get to know each other better, a chance to discuss the presentation with a group and raise questions, and refreshments. Many of our current members, and most of our leaders, point to this course as a pivotal time for them in their spiritual journey when they were first coming into our church.[4]

However you decide to do it, it is important that every congregation develop an appropriate way to help newcomers examine the faith and decide whether they would like to respond to the gospel invitation to enter the kingdom of God and become followers (disciples) of Jesus.

Having thought about how we can help people grow toward spiritual maturity as disciples of Jesus (the previous chapter) and how we can welcome and assimilate newcomers into our congregations and help them get started on this journey of discipleship and spiritual growth (this chapter), we are now in a position to move beyond simply greeting those who walk in; we can now go out actively seeking others to join us (the next two chapters).

FRIENDS AND FAMILY OF MEMBERS

The third category of people your congregation can influence consists of the members' friends and relatives who are not associated with any church community. Almost every church member will have friends, relatives, and acquaintances who are not involved in the life of any congregation or living their lives in the context of a vital faith. These networks of friendship represent an incredible opportunity for every congregation to share the good news and to influence people toward Christ.

It is a simple fact that the majority of people who were once outsiders to the church, but who are now growing disciples, were originally brought into the church and influenced toward Christ by a trusted friend or relative. People will more often trust a friend in this process than they will a stranger.

It makes sense then to believe that the most

> *The most effective way for any congregation to connect with outsiders and begin to influence them toward Christ is to work through the friendship networks of the members.*

effective way for any congregation to connect with outsiders and begin to influence them toward Christ is to work through the friendship networks of the members. For any congregation seeking to reach more people, these networks represent, by far, the greatest opportunities and potential. People invited in this way are also usually far easier to assimilate into the life of the congregation for the simple reason that the member who invited them will usually take responsibility for making sure their friend is feeling welcomed and included and is aware of the various possibilities for connecting more deeply with the congregation.

Keeping in mind our desire to help people become committed disciples, our process in this case is:

- Invite them to experience the church
- Welcome and assimilate them into the congregational community
- Disciple them toward spiritual maturity as committed followers of Jesus.

The Inviting Congregation

What we want to do is make the act of inviting a core value in our congregations. We want it to become a normal part of congregational life. We want to encourage our members to talk about the church and their faith as a normal part of their lives and everyday conversation. We want to be continually reminding them to think about whom they might be able to invite and celebrating this when it happens.

But getting members to invite their friends and relatives is not as easy as it might seem. We cannot assume that our members will begin to invite their friends and relatives simply because we point out the potential this category represents. There are usually a number of subtle factors at work that intimidate people and keep them from becoming enthusiastic inviters.[1]

For example, when leading workshops on faith sharing and inviting, I have frequently asked people, "How many of you have ever read a good book, or found a nice restaurant, or seen a good movie that you have then recommended to a friend?" Inevitably, almost everyone present raises his or her hand. I then go on to ask, "So then, if you know how to recommend books, or restaurants, or movies to your friends, why is it so difficult for you to recommend your church to them?"

The answer usually comes back quickly, "Because it is not the same. When I recommend a book, or a restaurant, or a movie, my friends take it as an act of friendship because they know I am trying to add value and enjoyment to their lives. But I am afraid that if I suggest they come to church with me they might think that I am suggesting that there is something wrong with them, that somehow I perceive that they are not good people, or that perhaps I consider myself to be morally superior to them." Obviously we are not suggesting anything of the sort when we invite a friend to church, and this is an easy obstacle to deal with, but my point is that there are many assumptions and perceptions of the church and Christian faith in the minds of people (both inside and outside the church) that intimidate Christians and make them reluctant to invite.

> *We want to encourage our members to talk about the church and their faith as a normal part of their lives and everyday conversation.*

Our goal of course is to help transform our congregations into evangelizing communities with members who are willing, and even enthusiastic, to share their faith within their circles of influence and invite people to come into the life of the church. But the average church member is usually going to need some help with this before he or she can become an enthusiastic inviter. In my experience, there are normally three key elements involved in helping a typical congregation become more enthusiastic and intentional in actively inviting others to join them.

First of all, we have to help them grow in their understanding and commitment to the point where they actually want to do so. Second, we have to show them how, so they are able to. Third, we have to remove the culture barrier in our congregation so they are willing to.

When we have a congregation of growing disciples who want to invite others, who know how to invite others and who are willing to invite others, there is a very real possibility that good things can happen.

Help Them Grow So They Want To

Again, we come back to the issue of discipleship and say once more that this is the single most important key to congregational transformation. A congregation can only be as good, as strong, as effective, as its ability to develop disciples. Without intentional discipleship training it is highly unlikely that a typical inwardly focused congregation can be transformed into an outwardly focused congregation.

> *With so many societal, institutional, and personal factors working to intimidate them, people are not going to step out and become inviters until they really want to, and no amount of external pressure is going to change this.*

People will not become enthusiastic inviters just because the congregational leaders think it is a good idea. With so many societal, institutional, and personal factors working to intimidate them, people are not going to step out and become inviters until they really want to, and no amount of external pressure is going to change this.

Unless people are being trained in discipleship this inner change will not take place. For one thing, it is unlikely that they will understand the importance of helping others come to faith. They will simply assume that church life is for those who go in for that sort of thing and that those who are interested will be quite capable of finding their own way into the church. Or they might suspect that the drive to reach others is about "empire building," or the old "bigger is better" syndrome, or about recruiting "new hands to share in the work," or "new giving units" to help out with the bills.

Furthermore, if they are not being helped to grow up in their faith, it is unlikely that they will feel that their faith is worth sharing or that they have a sufficient grasp on it to risk even starting a conversation that might drift in that direction. As one participant in a workshop said when we were discussing some of the reasons people might be reluctant or feel intimidated about initiating faith-centered conversations, "I just have a strong sense that I might be opening a real can of worms." When pressed a little further she explained that she felt she might be opening up a conversation that she was not really equipped to handle and could end up embarrassing herself.

To return to the earlier example of recommending a restaurant to friends, she knew that in doing so she would not be asked why she bothered to go to restaurants at all, or why she was interested in eating, or called upon to explain the process of digestion and prove that she understands how food is able to nourish her. But church is not like this at all. The fear is that if I invite a friend to church, I might well be asked why I attend church, what I believe, and what my reasons are for doing so. This might lead to a challenge to my beliefs, or to a series of questions or objections that I simply cannot answer. This could be embarrassing. Perhaps worse, it might lead to friction and hard feelings, which could pose a danger to an enjoyable friendship. All things considered, this person concludes, it is probably best just to leave this alone.

> *True evangelism is always the overflow of a life that is growing deeply into Christ.*

But growing disciples come to understand, in the course of their growth, that there is an outward dynamic at the very heart of the gospel: This good news is for sharing, and it is the commission and mandate of the church to share it as widely as possible. As their understanding of what it means to be the people of God expands and deepens, they become more acutely aware of the missionary thrust that permeates every page of the New Testament. With good training and teaching, they begin to develop eyes for "the harvest" that Jesus talked about (Matt. 9:37 and John 4:35) and to understand how important this work of sharing the gospel is to God and for the world.

As their own relationship with God is cultivated and nourished, as they begin to grow strong in their faith, and as they desire more and more to "find out what pleases the Lord" (Eph. 5:10) and to "live a life worthy of the calling" (Eph. 4:1), they find themselves thinking about what faithfulness in this matter of sharing the good news might look like for them.

As they continue to experience the work of God in their lives and to discover the depths of the riches of Christ, they will find themselves wanting to help others discover what they have found. True evangelism is always the overflow of a life that is growing deeply into Christ. The first step in developing an inviting congregation is to help them grow so they want to. Lasting change is always an inside job; the desire must come from within.

Teach Them So They Are Able

Even people who have the inner desire to be inviters and to witness effectively to their faith need some help in doing so. The second step in developing a witnessing and inviting congregation is to train them so they are able to witness and invite.[2] They need confidence and support in this so they don't feel as though they have been left on their own to twist in the wind.

As they become aware of the importance of sharing their faith with those who are still outside, and find that they are developing a desire to do so, they usually have at least these three questions about what this involves:

- Where should I start?
- What should I say?
- How should I say it?

Where Should I Start?

Start with those with whom you already enjoy friendship and personal respect. You might eventually get to the point where you can have such conversations with strangers (or you might not), but the place to begin is with those you already know.

The two important questions to ask ourselves here are, Do I have a faith worth sharing? and Do I have a friend worth sharing it with?[3]

Most people have family members, business associates, and acquaintances from their neighborhood and social circle with whom they enjoy friendship, respect, and a certain degree of personal influence.

In helping people think about where they might start inviting people to your church, suggest they begin here. Who do they know in each of these three areas who is not currently attending a church on a regular basis? Encourage them to pray for these people and to ask God to provide them with opportunities for faith-related conversations and opportunities to invite them to church.

What Should I Say?

Tell them about your church and what you like about it. Tell them how it adds value to your life and why you think they might like it or find it helpful too. Invite them to give it a try.

Think in terms of the question, What is the good news about my church that I think would be helpful to share with my friends? What does this church offer that, from their point of view, would make it worth their while to try us out?

If the conversation leads on to a deeper discussion about the Christian faith, as it well might, try to think in terms of the question, What is the good news about Jesus that I have experienced and would like to share? The point in such conversations is not to get involved in deep theological or philosophical discussions (which are rarely productive in terms of helping people come to faith) but rather to share as simply and directly as possible what Jesus has done in your life and why you recommend him to others. Never underestimate the power of sharing your personal faith story with another. It is by far the most effective evangelistic method there is, and it is within the reach of every growing Christian!

Telling Your Story

Many people, in thinking of how they might outline their faith story in order to be able to share it clearly and simply, find it helpful to think in terms of three main focal points, which can function in a way as the three chapters of their story.

Chapter One: My Life Before Turning to Christ. This chapter includes some reflection on the type of person I was when I was living outside of a vital faith and did not think of myself as a committed follower of Jesus. In this part of the story, I will want to say something about what my life was like, what I was living for, what I valued, what my worldview was like, how it was formed, and so on. I might even want to say something about my understanding of and feelings about Christianity, the church, and even religion in general.

Chapter Two: How I Met Christ. This chapter focuses on the various circumstances and influences in my life that eventually led me to become a follower of Jesus. What were the issues that led me to consider him? What were the questions I had? Who were the people who played influential roles in this process as I came to place my trust in Jesus and step out to follow him? What did this process look like and feel like?

Chapter Three: My Life with Christ. In this chapter we attempt to describe something of the difference it has made in my life to become an intentional follower of Jesus. How am I different from the person described in chapter one? How has it changed me as a spouse, as a parent, as a worker, as a friend, as a citizen? How have my goals and values changed? What difference has it made in my behavior? What are some of the challenges I face? What is my growing edge in this?

An Alternative Version

It is important to point out here that the previous outline does not fit the experience of many deeply committed and growing

Christians. These are the people whose experience of the Christian faith is such that they cannot recall a time when they did not know themselves to be connected with Jesus and open to his presence in their lives. Such people are blessed indeed! In their case the three chapters read differently, perhaps something like this:

Chapter One: Early Christian Influences in My Life. Rather than reflecting on life apart from Christ, this chapter usually tells of what it was like to grow up in a Christian home with parents (or a parent) who were committed to Christ and who taught their children from earliest childhood about the God who loves them and what Jesus has done for them. It might include the experience of being part of a church that took children seriously and helped them to worship and grow in their faith. It might include reflections on the comfort of Christ's presence in various situations and the security of being assured of God's love. What a wonderful thing it is to be able to include a chapter like this in your faith story. Many people who come to faith in later life dearly wish that they could tell this chapter instead.

Chapter Two: Making It My Own. For those who tell this version of the story, there is usually a period in adolescence or early adulthood when they have to go through the process of owning the faith for themselves. They become aware that they cannot go on forever on the faith of their parents and their church community; they are now responsible for the direction of their own life, and there are important choices to make. This sometimes (but not always) includes some serious wrestling with issues and choices as they consider what their life will be about.

Chapter Three: My Life with Christ Today. As in the first version, this chapter focuses on what it means for me today to be a follower of Jesus and how my faith influences the way I think and live.

Churches seeking to develop a witnessing and inviting membership should make a point of encouraging their members to tell their faith stories to one another and of providing plenty of opportunities for them to do so. They should seek to make this a normal and expected part of congregational life. In worship services, at committee meetings, at social events, in all sorts of meetings and courses, devise ways for people to spend some time hearing one another's stories.

As these stories are shared in various settings, an amazing thing happens: People become aware, in a deep way, that God is among them and that God is working in the lives of people they know. There is a reverence that develops as they become aware that they are standing on holy ground. This realization (which often comes as a surprise) that God is in fact among them and has been working in their lives, and in the lives of people they know is a tremendous encouragement to the whole church. I don't know of anything that has the potential for boosting congregational morale and enthusiasm as quickly and as powerfully as this simple act of storytelling does.

It is also worth noting that the experience of telling these stories with others in the church provides the opportunity for practice in a friendly setting before setting out to tell them outside to people who might still be somewhat skeptical.

A Gospel Outline

Remember that the point of the conversation we are imagining here is to invite our friends and relatives to consider trying our church, with the hope that this invitation might eventually prove to be a part of the process through which they come to faith in Christ and join us in the journey of discipleship. We have recognized, however, that this invitation might well lead to a discussion in which we get a chance to tell the story of what Jesus has done for us personally and why we are interested in helping others get to know him. We want to be prepared for this.

Sometimes the conversation might even go beyond this, and we will find ourselves being asked more substantial questions like, What is Christianity all about anyway? or Just what is it that you people actually believe? At such times it is helpful to have a short and simple gospel outline to fall back on. Many such outlines have been developed to help people with these evangelizing opportunities. The one I like to use builds around a number of words beginning with the letter R.

The first R stands for the word *relationship*. It is important to point out to inquirers that Christianity is not really about religious rules, rites, or rituals but is about a relationship. We have been created for a personal, interactive, deeply intimate relationship with God. This, in fact, is at the heart of what it means to be human. It is this relationship, Christians believe, that is at the heart of every spiritual quest.

But this relationship has sustained terrible damage due to the pernicious influence of evil working throughout the world seeking to corrupt and destroy God's good creation. With this relationship damaged, our inner natural tendency is to try to keep God safely at arm's length rather than welcome him into the center of our lives. It just seems like good sense. In other words, rather than enjoying intimacy with God, we are now in a state of alienation from God. The relationship has broken down.

The second R stands for the word *reconciliation*. The good news of the gospel is that God's love is far greater than our fear or alienation. Even when we are fearful, indifferent, or downright hostile toward God, God still loves us more than we love ourselves. In Jesus, God has come to show us, in human terms, what God is really like and how much God cares for us. Through the death and resurrection of Jesus, God has dealt (in ways we can never comprehend) with the power of evil and the reality of sin and offers us the opportunity to make a fresh start in life, living in friendship with him and learning to live as we were created to do.

The third R in this simple outline stands for the word *reign*. *Reign* refers to the "reign of God," or in more biblical language the "kingdom of God." What is in mind here is the world as God intends it to be, a world in which, as Jesus taught us to pray, God's will is done, just as it is in heaven. This is God's vision for creation, history, and humanity; it is the vision that in God's good time will be the only reality. As those who have been reconciled to God through Jesus, and have become disciples, our goal is to begin learning to live the life of this kingdom now. We acknowledge the reign of God in our lives and begin the adventure of letting this new perspective and adventure touch and inform every area of life.

You never know where a simple conversation about the gospel might lead. My own experience has confirmed in me the conviction that there are many people who are willing to listen to a short and clear explanation of the gospel from a trusted and respected friend sharing humbly, honestly, and from the heart. The truth is that there are far more people who are willing to listen than there are Christians who are willing or able to make the presentation.

How Should I Say It?

The short answer to this, of course, is to say it graciously, lovingly, and sensitively. Avoid any appearance of condescension, speak in a natural voice (not preachy), and avoid getting into arguments. Again, it is a simple fact that people are loved into God's kingdom far more often, and far more easily, than they are argued in. Any time the conversation seems to be developing an edge, back off graciously and return to the conversation at another time.

Remember that faith-related conversations should be genuine dialogue in which we are interested in listening as well as speaking. Ask lots of questions, seeking to discover their attitudes toward Christianity and the church, their past experiences of church and Christian people, their beliefs about the purpose of life, where they got those beliefs, and what they believe to be the most important questions about life. Asking such questions and being willing to listen will often lead to a fascinating and productive conversation.

> *There are many pressures at work, some subtle and some not so subtle, that intimidate people and steal their enthusiasm for speaking about their faith and their church.*

It is also a good idea always to ask permission before beginning to talk with them about such matters. This is as simple as saying something like, "I'm sorry your experience of the church has been so unhelpful. My experience is quite different. I attend a church that I really enjoy, and I'd love to tell you about it if you are interested." This simple act of asking permission can go a long way toward opening up a good conversation.

The Unspoken Question

In addition to the three questions outlined above, many people have a fourth (often unspoken) question about this matter of faith sharing and inviting.

"Why," they find themselves wondering, "do I feel so uneasy about this? Even though I understand how important it is and have been given some help in how to do it, I still feel uneasy. Why?" Perhaps they even feel guilty about it. "What is wrong with me?" they might wonder. "If only I were a better Christian," or "If only I had more faith, I wouldn't be so reluctant." The truth is that most people do have a certain inner reluctance or hesitation about the prospect of actually seeking to initiate faith-related, inviting conversations.

In a society such as ours there are many reasons why people feel uneasy about this. There are many pressures at work, some subtle and some not so subtle, that intimidate people and steal their enthusiasm for speaking about their faith and their church. Rather than berate them for their timidity in this area, which might well produce feelings of guilt and inadequacy but rarely lead to behavioral change, it is better to acknowledge these factors openly and to help people deal with them.

Some people, for example, have been led to believe that because our society places a high value on mutual tolerance and pluralism, giving everyone the right to live and believe as they choose, that we should therefore not be attempting to persuade others to our way of thinking and believing. Two things need to be said about this immediately.

The first is that pluralism is not the same as relativism, although the one can quickly shade into the second if we are not careful. Pluralism says that everyone has the right to believe as they choose. Relativism says that ultimately it doesn't matter which set of beliefs a person chooses because they are all of equal value. As Christians we can willingly embrace the concept of pluralism, but the particularity and uniqueness of the claims about Christ do not allow us to embrace relativism.

The second is that it is important to help people understand that it is a very immature and fragile type of pluralism that demands that people not be allowed to speak openly about the things they value most and believe most deeply because they might offend others who see things differently. What is really needed, if pluralism is to be of any value at all in society, is a mature pluralism that recognizes the value of people being able to discuss openly and passionately the issues that are most important to them, and yes, even to persuade others to change their way of thinking. What is required here of course is grace, civility, sensitivity, respect, and the ability to make your case winsomely and with integrity.

Many Christians have a misconception that unchurched people have carefully thought through the claims of the Christian faith and, after deep soul searching and wrestling, have rejected it on intellectual grounds.

This is simply not the case. The truth is that the great majority of people around us have hardly any understanding at all about the faith, and what information they do have is often shaky, hazy, and confused. Christians rightly sense that a conversation about their church might well turn into a discussion of Christianity and that some interesting questions will be raised, but they should be helped to understand that these conversations present a wonderful opportunity to help people understand the faith more clearly and clear up some common misunderstandings.

Some have also picked up the idea somewhere along the line that faith-related conversations should be primarily about sin. They fear that their role in such conversations is to tell people they are sinners and to get them to admit this. No wonder they feel reluctant to move a conversation in this direction. But this is not what witnessing and inviting are all about. Encourage them to stress the relational aspect of the faith instead, helping people to see that God loves them and is inviting them to a closer relationship. Encourage them to tell their friends what they like about their church and why they think they might find it helpful or enjoyable as well. Remember to help them think in terms of the question, What is the good news about my church that I would like to share with others?

Remove the Culture Barrier So They Are Willing To

Even for growing Christians who genuinely desire to see others come to faith and who have been helped to develop some confidence and enthusiasm about initiating faith-related conversations, there is another major consideration that needs to be addressed. If they are going to invite their friends, we must remove the culture barrier so they are willing to do so.[4]

The point here is that people must be proud of their church and genuinely believe that their friends will enjoy it, or they will not invite them. The test here is how they think they would feel in church if they had brought a friend who was sitting beside them. This is sometimes uncharitably described as the "cringe factor."

> *People must be proud of their church and genuinely believe that their friends will enjoy it, or they will not invite them.*

It is an instructional exercise to sit through a typical service in your church and view it through newcomers' eyes. What would they see? What would they hear? What would they feel? How would you feel if one of your unchurched friends were sitting beside you in this service? Would you be proud? Or would you be feeling a bit uneasy, perhaps a little squirmish at times? What would you be proud of? What would you be uneasy about? One thing that we can count on for sure is that people are not going to invite their friends to church if they feel there is any chance that they will be embarrassed by doing so. This is a plain and simple fact.

Everything that was said in chapter 2 concerning those who walk in on Sunday mornings applies here as well. Church members want to be sure that their friends will receive a warm welcome when they show up and will be treated as though they really matter. They need to be confident that they will feel included and that they will be able to understand and enjoy what is going on. At the same time, they won't want them to be overwhelmed and intimidated, feeling that they are being rushed and hustled into something for which they are not yet ready.

It is important to emphasize here that in speaking of making our churches more accessible to newcomers, in seeking to create a climate in which they will feel more at ease and less threatened, we are not talking about "watering down" the gospel to make it something that so-called modern people can accept. Nothing could be further from the truth.

If we are unable to connect with them, or if our churches are places from which they desire to flee as quickly as possible, or if our members would be embarrassed even to invite them, there is no chance at all that we will ever be able to help them come to faith. As those who have been entrusted with the gospel, it is our responsibility to remove every possible barrier from our side, in order to connect with and be able to influence them.

The style of worship most likely to connect with people today will be both celebrational and relational in tone. In times gone by, the more usual style of worship sought to emphasize the transcendence and holiness of God and tended to be more formal and solemn, teaching people to walk circumspectly and to be respectful in God's presence. By contrast, a service that is more casual and informal in nature, featuring an equally legitimate emphasis on intimacy with God and the fel-

> *We are trying to create a climate in which they can hear the gospel in a way that connects with them, and opens them up to the possibility of a life-changing relationship with Jesus Christ.*

lowship of his people, is more likely to connect with the people we are seeking to reach today.

Such a service will be more inspirational than somber. It will be uplifting. It will be filled with good news and hope. It is a fact of life that people love celebrations and, given the choice, most prefer a party to a funeral! Many people are carrying heavy loads, living lives characterized by busyness and stress. They are likely to tell you, if asked, that they already have enough heaviness in their lives and that they don't need a church to give them more. On the other hand, a church that could help them understand and deal with their stresses and issues might prove very attractive.

True joy and celebration in the midst of the stresses of life is what they need and crave. Churches that are able to attract people, and to which their members are proud to invite their friends, are generally churches that have learned to celebrate the good news of the gospel in their worship. It is good to remember that people who are just beginning to enter church life probably leave the service reflecting at least as much on how they felt during the service as on what they learned.

But they would want to feel as though they had learned something too. So it is important to ask, Would they have been able to understand what was going on, or would they have felt like they had happened upon some form of life from another planet? Would they understand the language that was used? If not, they probably won't stick around long enough to learn it; more important, members won't invite their friends if

> *Churches that are able to attract people, and to which their members are proud to invite their friends, are generally churches that have learned to celebrate the good news of the gospel in their worship.*

they fear that this might be the case. And if they did understand, would it make any difference to them? Would they have heard something that offered the possibility of adding real value to their lives and making a difference?

We have to remember that there is more to good preaching and teaching than just presenting the truth. In addition to, Is this the truth? they are probably also asking, What's the point of this; why should this be important to me? Good communication always connects faith and life, helping people make sense of life and offering guidance on how to live. In addition to dealing with the ultimate questions of life, preaching that adds value to people's lives helps them make it through an ordinary day, dealing in healthy ways with all the challenges that life throws our way. Paul Hiebert calls these the "middle issues" and cautions that churches that neglect to offer counsel and guidance with these issues miss a wonderful opportunity to influence people with the gospel.[5]

Courage Required

It requires tremendous courage for a congregation to begin to ask serious questions about the culture barrier. There is a good chance that it will lead them into uncomfortable territory. But these questions must be asked if the church is to move ahead.

The basic question here is, Do the members of your church regularly invite their unchurched friends and relatives to give your church a try? If not, why not?

Do their answers to these questions have anything to do with the culture barrier? If so, try asking them, What type of church do you think you might feel more at ease about inviting your friends and family to? What would such a church look like? What would it offer? What would it do? This could open up a productive line of thought.

On the other hand, if they do invite their friends and family, when they come, do they stay, or is one or two visits usually the limit? Again, it would be interesting to pursue the question *why*.

These questions are very likely to lead to a consideration of that dreaded word *change*. But the changes required in removing the culture barrier cannot be imposed from without. They can only come when a significant group of people, under wise leadership, are growing to the point where they are willingly asking,

What could we do that would make us more effective in reaching outsiders? What are we currently doing that helps in this area? What are some of the things that work against us? And of course, the most important question of all, What price are we willing to pay in order to become more effective in connecting with outsiders? In congregational life, the first rule of change is always this: Only those who are themselves being changed can willingly embrace change for the sake of others.

Two Realities

When we have done our best to encourage and equip our people to share their faith and invite others into the life of our church, two realities will remain.

The first is that many, perhaps even most, will rarely ever get to the point where they have a real faith-sharing conversation of the kind outlined above. Those outlines are offered mainly to give them confidence that they can rise to the occasion, should the opportunity arise. For the majority, the closest they will ever get to this is to invite a friend or neighbor to something that is going on at the church that they think they might enjoy. It follows that the more creative we can be in offering events in addition to Sunday worship to which people can invite their friends the more successful we will be in encouraging our members to become intentional about inviting.

The second reality is that, even when we have done our best to remove the culture barrier and to offer other events to which people can invite their friends, for many of these friends it will simply be too big a stretch to agree to come to a church event. In this case it might be helpful for people to think about inviting one or more friends to a social event in their home, which will also be attended by others from the church. This is a good halfway strategy to help the unchurched get to know some church people and to enjoy their company. As the members talk enthusiastically and naturally about the church and as they befriend the unchurched in such situations, it is possible that the initial fears and resistance will begin to fade and smooth the way for a timely invitation to join us at church.

In the next chapter we are going to consider some of the factors that influence a church's ability to attract people toward it—what I like to call a church's "magnetic field." At this point it is appropriate to point out that of all the factors influencing this magnetic field, the enthusiasm of the current members and their willingness to invite is by far the strongest. Churches that want to share the good news as widely as possible put a lot of effort into developing witnessing and inviting members.

CHAPTER FIVE

THOSE WHO LIVE IN THE NEIGHBORHOOD

The fourth category of people your congregation can influence consists of those who live in the neighborhood surrounding your church. Chances are these people know your church exists because they pass it on a regular basis as they go about their daily routines, but they hardly, if ever, think about it. They have no connection with your church in any significant way, either through your programmers or your members. Your church, though close by, is not on their radar screens.

Once again, we remind ourselves that our ultimate goal is to equip people to live to the glory of God. With this in mind, the process for influencing this fourth category is:

- Connect with them
- Invite them
- Welcome and assimilate them
- Disciple them toward spiritual maturity as committed followers of Jesus

Given the fact that you have no contact with these people, this represents a significant challenge. In fact, for the majority of congregations, this category will probably prove to be the most difficult to influence in any significant way. It is important to recognize this because many congregations never get around to developing a serious, well-thought-out strategy for reaching these people. They simply assume that this group, of all people, should simply find their way into the church on their own. After all, they are our neighbors. In fact, some congregations actually seem to be annoyed with these people for not doing so, as though they are somehow not being cooperative!

The most common strategy for reaching those who live in the neighborhood seems to be the church sign. After all, it says that everyone is welcome and states clearly what time the service begins. But this is hardly an effective strategy. The day is long gone when people would show up for church simply because it is there and they live in the neighborhood.

Looking at It from Their Point of View

With regard to my own congregation, I sometimes sit down and remind myself of who actually lives in my neighborhood and what their lives are like. I try to imagine a typical household within a ten- or fifteen-minute drive of our church that I would like for our congregation to be able to connect with and influence toward a vital faith in Jesus Christ and then ask what it might take for us to be able to do so.

A typical household within this radius of our church would probably consist of two parents and a couple of children. Of course, there are a great variety of household configurations, including single-parent families, empty nesters, seniors and singles of various ages (some young and never married, some older and never married, some young or middle-aged and divorced, and some widowed), but this two-parent, two-child household would be quite typical.

I am hoping that this family will come to church on Sunday morning. From my perspective as a pastor, that seems to be quite a simple thing; it certainly doesn't seem to be asking too much. I know that it would be good for them if they did, and having attended church for most of my life, I can't imagine what might be holding them back.

But when I think like this I am making a mistake, one that far too many congregations make on a regular basis. I am looking at the situation from my point of view, not theirs. Everyone involved in marketing knows that in order to influence people you have to look at the situation from their point of view before you look at it from yours. Remember Rick Warren's observation that if you want to catch a fish you have to think like a fish.

In the family that I am imagining, both parents are university educated with responsible and demanding jobs. In the previous week, perhaps one or both of them has spent a day or two out of town on business. They have brought work home from the office to be done in the evening, the children have been involved in various activities, and meals have been taken on the run. By the time the weekend rolls around, everyone is exhausted. Friday night might be spent just vegging out in front of the TV.

Saturday is the day for catching up with everything that needs to be done around the house. Household cleaning and laundry, preparing some meals for the coming week, grocery shopping, yard work, household maintenance, children's activities, and more take up the better part of the day. By Saturday evening they may be starting to feel as though their life is almost under control again, and maybe they even have a little energy for some nondemanding recreational or social activity. But then again, maybe not.

Now comes Sunday morning. I would like to see them in church. But looking at it from their point of view what are their options? Or, to put it somewhat more bluntly, what am I competing with? For starters, they might well prefer to do nothing instead of doing anything, including go to church. They could sit around in their pajamas and robes, enjoying the fact that there are no pressing appointments today. The kids could sit in front of the television in their pajamas, eating cereal and watching cartoons, happy that they just lie around for a couple of hours. Mom and dad can enjoy a second cup of coffee while they read the paper, or they might well decide just to stay in bed. They need some time just to reconnect with each other. This might be the only time of the week when they are not too utterly stressed and exhausted to enjoy making love. (I might be able to plan a great church service, but it is going to have to be really good to compete with that!)

> *Vital congregations have learned to ask, How can we support the people in this neighborhood? rather than, How can we get the people in this neighborhood to support us?*

But their busyness is not the only thing working against me in my desire to see this family come into my church. In addition to the frenetic pace of their lives, the family might have some assumptions about the church that would hinder them from ever moving toward us. If the subject of church ever came up, they might express the opinion that the church is just after their money or that it will make huge demands on their time if they get too close. These assumptions are commonplace in our culture.

Leaving aside for the moment the question of where these assumptions might come from, the family I am describing here know that they are already spending 125 percent of their income, that they simply have no time to give anyone, and that time and finances are the greatest source of stress in their lives. Furthermore, without having given it much serious thought, they might also express the opinion that whatever it is that the church teaches has been debunked a long time ago and is no longer worthy of consideration by intelligent people.

Finding a Point of Access: What's in It for Me?

When I look at things from this perspective I can see immediately what a formidable challenge it will be to connect with this family and be able to influence them toward faith in Jesus Christ. Perhaps the most important thing to remember in all of this is that if they ever do start thinking about coming to church, they will be thinking in terms of, What is in it for me? and What is the church offering that would make it worth my while? Their question will never be, I wonder if there's a church anywhere in this neighborhood that could use a little help from us? Vital congregations have learned to ask, How can we support the people in this neighborhood? rather than, How can we get the people in this neighborhood to support us?

The questions we need to keep in mind when thinking about this category then are, If we are able to connect with them, what would we like to see happen in their lives as a result of their involvement with us? and What are we offering that, from their point of view, would make it worthwhile for them to consider becoming involved with us? We need to be thinking about how to connect with them and why we want to connect with them. Sometimes in the busyness of church life it is possible to lose focus and to forget that our bottom line is always changed lives as we help people come to faith and grow toward maturity as followers of Jesus.

What then might be the possible points of connection with people such as those described above? Where in all this hurry and possible skepticism are there points of access to the gospel? What do we have to offer that is in keeping with our mandate to be the church and that might be of interest to them?

> *People who move toward the church generally do so for two major reasons: to learn about God and to find some guidance and direction for living.*

It is helpful to keep in mind here that people who move toward the church generally do so for two reasons: to learn about God and to find some guidance and direction for living. (We know of course that they usually stay in a church if they have managed to make some good friends and have found a place that helps them feel as though they are contributing to something that is truly worthwhile, but these are not what usually brings them in.)

One of the characteristics of our culture in recent years is an increasing interest in spirituality. A quick visit to any popular bookstore will bear this out. It seems as though we have collectively come to a place where we realize that the thoroughgoing materialism of past decades and the deeply entrenched rationalism of the past few centuries are not adequate to nourish us inwardly as human beings. There is a spiritual thirst in the culture as we come to realize that the acquisition of things cannot bring inner fulfillment and that there are forms of truth that rationalism cannot carry. If the busyness and skepticism described above pose a challenge for the church, this renewed interest in spirituality presents us with opportunities beyond our wildest imaginings!

It is worth revisiting the scenario outlined above and probing a little more deeply. On the surface, that might have looked like an impossible situation. There is simply no room or time in that lifestyle for considering, let alone cultivating, a life of faith and discipleship. But things are not always what they seem on the surface. Chances are, that late at night or in rare moments of quiet and solitude, one or both of these adults have found themselves wondering what it is all about and are finding it difficult to come up with satisfying answers. They are beginning to sense that in the hurry and pressure of making a living, life itself is passing them by. Are they missing something, they wonder? Is there more to it all than making a living and getting ahead?

Or perhaps they are beginning to worry a little about their children. They have a sense that they should be giving them some teaching in ethics and morals and spirituality, but they don't know how. They might remember their own childhood visits to church or Sunday school and feel that their children might be being shortchanged in an important area of life. They want to be good people; they want their children to be good people; they want to live respectable, responsible, worthwhile lives. They want a good marriage and a strong, loving family. But they sense that they are missing the center around which all of this can be organized and out of which it can grow. Perhaps they had even hoped that their marriage would be this center, but in the stress of life they are discovering that it can't carry this weight, and it is beginning to feel the strain of overload.

Where these questions are beginning to form and these yearnings beginning to grow there is a point of access for the gospel. Such people are moving in the direction of a spiritual quest. As Christians, of course, we believe that when these questions and yearnings begin to arise, the spirit of God is at work in their lives, preparing the soil to receive the seed of the gospel. Of course this doesn't mean that their search is going to bring them to church. That is still a big step, and there are many spiritualities on offer out there that have little or nothing to do with the gospel, but it does mean that a church that has given this some thought might eventually be in a position to connect with them. Can your church help them to learn about God? Can your church offer them some direction and guidance for living?

Saying that people should move toward the church in order to learn about God does not go far enough. In reality they are looking for a lot more than information about God

> *Where these questions are beginning to form and these yearnings beginning to grow there is a point of access for the gospel.*

or about how this particular congregation or denomination thinks about God. They are actually seeking an experience of God. Chances are, when they come into one of your services, they go home asking, What did I feel? before they ask, What did I learn? Their antennae are out, trying to discern whether or not they are getting a sense that God can actually be encountered in this place among these people. Churches with truly inspiring worship have a much better chance of connecting with these people than churches that give the impression of simply going through the motions or being settled into a comfortable, perhaps even tired, routine.

Similarly, in saying that people move toward the church seeking guidance and direction for living does not mean that they are looking for rules and regulations to be imposed upon their lives.

They are looking for that sense of center that will give place and meaning to every area of their lives, a vital core that defines who they are, what their lives are about, and from which the rest of their lives develop and are nourished. They are not looking to add a religious dimension to an already hectic existence; they are looking for a stream that can flow through every part of their busy life, refreshing them, nurturing them, and helping them to get things under control.

They are looking for the truth that lies behind all of life and that gives every part of life its meaning. And they are looking for a place that can help them make the everyday connections between faith and life—their life—and so help them to live healthy, meaningful, worthwhile lives in healthy households and relationships.

If we cannot do this for them, the issue of whether or not the gospel is true will ultimately hold little interest for them. They will decide for themselves whether or not it is true once they have determined whether or not it works.

On the other hand, when a church is actually doing this, the word tends to get around. A church that is able to help people discover the joyful adventure of kingdom living is a church that can meet these people at the point of their search.

The key to influencing this category then is to know what you want to see happen in their lives, to understand that your best chance of influencing them is by meeting them at the point of their spiritual yearnings, and by having something practical to offer that they will perceive to be of value in this regard. It is counterproductive to try to connect with them before we are clear about what we have to offer. One of the problems I have with many church advertising campaigns is that if they are successful in attracting some unchurched people, those people will immediately remember why they drifted away from church in the first place and will become hardened against future efforts to reach them.

This is why it is so important to have done our work carefully in the previous categories before attempting to reach out and connect with this group.

- When our worship is truly inspiring, our welcome warm and our path to assimilation clear.
- When we are able to offer opportunities to under-stand the gospel clearly and to make relevant connec-tions to everyday life.
- When we are able to introduce people simply and passionately to the adventure of kingdom living.
- When our members, themselves enthusiastic and growing disciples, are able to speak well of our church and share in natural language the difference that faith in Jesus and membership in this church means in their lives.

Then we are ready to think about how we can best connect with those who live around us, confident that we are offering something of great value that will refresh and enrich their lives.

Examining Your Magnetic Field

In seeking to connect with those who live in the vicinity of your church, it is important to understand that every congrega-tion has a magnetic field which represents its ability to attract people into its sphere of influence. The strength and range of this magnetic field varies from congregation to congregation, but the essential elements are the same for all. These include:

- your buildings
- your advertising
- your services
- your reputation
- your members' comments

These are the key factors informing the impression your neighbors will have of your church, and each of them plays a role in determining your capacity to draw people in and influence them with the gospel.

Your Buildings

Location obviously makes a difference. A church building located on a major traffic route will clearly be more visible than one that is tucked away on a side street. There is not much that can be said about this. Your location is your location, unless you are prepared to get involved in a major effort to relocate. That might be a good idea for many congregations, but such considerations go well beyond the scope of this book.

Whatever your location, the condition of your grounds and buildings is extremely important. For many people passing by, the condition of your property is all they know about you. Tidy grounds and well-maintained buildings speak well of a congregation; buildings in obvious need of repair and maintenance and grounds that are in need of some loving care do not. It is as simple as that. Unfortunately, sometimes congregations can become so familiar with their facilities that they no longer notice that they are in need of care. They would be surprised to hear that people find them unattractive.

It is a good idea to walk around on a regular basis and consciously try to look at your buildings and property through the eyes of an outsider. What have you grown accustomed to that would immediately stand out to a newcomer seeing it for the first time? Are there silent little messages anywhere that might attract or repel passersby? For example, a sign that says "Keep off the Lawn," or "Do Not Park Here" sends one message; a bench on the lawn with a sign that says "Sit Down and Rest Awhile" or a sign in the closest part of the parking lot that says "Reserved for First-Time Guests" sends another. All of these things are readily noticed by people passing by and help them form an impression of what your congregation may be like.

Does your building look accessible to potential newcomers? Is it clear where the main entrance is? Is the property well signed so that people can easily find their way around? Is it lit up at night, drawing attention to itself, or is it hidden away in the darkness. Many churches could immediately raise their profile in the

> *Every congregation has a few people who act like the whole point of church life is never to spend any money, but it is impossible to save your way into a thriving ministry.*

community with a few well-placed lights! Perhaps some in the congregation might regard this as an unnecessary expense, but it is money well spent. Every congregation has a few people who act like the whole point of church life is never to spend any money, but it is impossible to save your way into a thriving ministry. Healthy financial stewardship training, rather than frugality, is a much better way to financial health in a congregation.

The subject of church signs deserves a section all to itself, but here I just want to emphasize the importance of making sure that the sign is both visible and clear. Many signs look as though they are intended to be read by people either on foot or on horseback, rather than by people in cars. By far the greatest majority of church signs that I have seen use print that is much too small, and usually they are set up incorrectly, to be read by people standing in front of them, rather than approaching rapidly from either side. I have seen signs that are almost totally hidden by shrubbery, and even a sign that was facing the wrong way on a dead end street! I have seen signs that had incorrect information about the times of services (the explanation given was that we all know when the services begin anyway) and a sign that had no times on it at all. Two parishioners in my congregation reported on their efforts to attend a small church in a village near their summer vacation spot. It actually took them several weeks to be able to figure out when the services were held. But the sign assured them that they were welcome.

Many congregations might not be in a position to do anything about their location, but the maintenance of our buildings and property and the messages we send with and on our signs are matters that are under our control. In the final analysis, fixing up your building, tidying up the grounds, lighting the property at night, and getting a good clear sign won't start a revival or even create a flow of people to your church, but it is an important part of the overall process of creating a higher profile and making a good impression. Good buildings and clear signs may never attract anyone into your congregation, but poorly maintained facilities and careless signs will certainly keep them out. At the very least, getting this area under control will go a long way to boosting congregational morale, and that is indispensable for effective ministry.

Your Advertising

Advertising is about your efforts to let the community know that you are there and that you are open for business. What do you want to say to your community about who you are, what you are like, what you are about, and why it would be a good idea for them to check out what you have to offer? Furthermore, how do you want to say it? What would be the best method for getting your message out?

Aside from the church sign, for the majority of churches advertising is limited to a short statement in the yellow pages of the telephone book and perhaps a notice on the church page of the local paper. These are good places to have information about your church, but it is important to understand that these ads are not very effective in reaching the unchurched. They are mainly for Christian

> *Good buildings and clear signs may never attract anyone into your congregation; but poorly maintained facilities and careless signs will certainly keep them out.*

people who for any one of a variety of reasons are looking for a church in the area. I must admit that when I look at the church ads in our local papers, in most cases, I wonder who in the world they are intended for!

It might be a good idea in your congregation to form a marketing group consisting of people with enthusiasm and energy for this, to do some brainstorming and planning around how to let your neighborhood know what you are all about. Their thinking may include, but not be limited to, scheduling of direct mailings over the course of a year, setting up a website and including the website address on all church communications, posters and flyers distributed around town, articles about various aspects of your ministry in the local paper, and door to door visitations by your members.

In seeking to raise your congregational profile, are there events in your community that you can participate in that would let people know you are alive and open for business? Is there a local parade in which your church could enter a float that says something about who you are? Could you put benches at bus stops, indicating that this bench is courtesy of your congregation? Could you sponsor good citizenship and community service awards in the local schools and have representatives of your congregation present them to the winners at graduation?

A new congregation in my area created a real buzz with a series of extremely attractive doorknob hangers with which they blitzed the area on a regular basis. One offered "the top ten reasons why people don't go to church." The reasons were all quite humorous and probably struck a responsive chord with a lot of people; reason number one was, "Because they have never tried our church!" That church is welcoming a lot of first-time visitors on Sunday mornings.

I heard of one church whose members regularly visited in the neighborhood on Saturday mornings. When the householder answered the door they would introduce themselves as representatives of their church and say, "Today our prayer team is meeting to pray for the people on this street. We are just calling to inquire whether there is something specific in this household that you would like us to pray for?" Obviously many people were initially taken aback by this approach, but that church quickly developed a reputation for caring for those who live nearby, and many people sought it out for help. It also grew quickly!

We have made reference to the fact that people are looking for answers to the ultimate questions of life and also to the "middle issues" of how to live wisely and well. Perhaps you could develop a series of sermons that address either of these, give them creative titles, and advertise them around the neighborhood. At the very least this could let some of your neighbors know that you are thinking on the same wavelength as they are. The typical sermon titles encountered on the church page won't work, but a little brainstorming with this can pay huge dividends.

I was once in a city where I saw a huge billboard beside the main traffic route posing the question, "Have you ever wondered . . . " followed by a series of statements such as, "What true home improvement really is?" or "What happens to you ten minutes after you die?" or "What Jesus would say to Jo-Jo the Psychic?" (a popular TV personality in the area). This billboard was placed there by a local church, and these questions were the topics of a series of sermons about to be preached. The billboard gave the name and phone number of the church and the date on which each topic would be preached. In answer to my questions, I discovered that this church was enjoying significant growth. The word was spreading that they were dealing with significant issues with humor, and in a healthy, nonthreatening way.

Easter and Christmas are seasons of the year when people might be a little more open than usual to the possibility of attending a church service. You might want to consider taking advantage of this opportunity by planning some special event around this seasonal theme and advertising it around the community. Encourage your members to make a special point of mentioning it to their neighbors and relatives. Follow this up by planning a special series of sermons or scheduling a course that they might find helpful, like parenting, or financial planning, or exploring the faith. When they come to this event or service, make sure the next sermon series is well highlighted and invite everyone to come back. In our congregation we regularly plan such a sermon series (as well as one of our Christianity 101

courses) for the weeks immediately following Christmas
and Easter.

> *We should never advertise ourselves until we are sure that we have something worth advertising.*

The basic point here is to do whatever you can to let people know you are there. Use any and all means possible, tapping as deeply as you can into the creativity of your members, many of whom would be truly excited to be a part of such brainstorming. As in many other areas of church life, your best friend and biggest limitation in this is your collective imagination. My advice is to go for it, and be prepared to go over the edge and to color outside the lines. Make your advertising interesting; we already have far too many people convinced that church is too boring for them.

It goes without saying (but I will say it anyway, just to be sure) that a basic rule here is that we should never advertise ourselves until we are sure that we have something worth advertising. The problem with most initiatives that I have seen, with churches offering guest services or groups of churches mounting an advertising campaign, is that most of the churches involved aren't really ready for company. Many visitors will only be on site for five or ten minutes before they remember why it was they quit going to church in the first place! It will be even harder to connect with them the next time around.

Our advertising should not promise anything that we cannot deliver. Avoid making extravagant claims about yourself, but let people know that this is a place where they will be warmly welcomed, where their concerns will be taken seriously, and where, you believe, they will be offered something of significant value if they will only give you a chance.

Your Services

We noted earlier that in looking at the neighborhood around our churches and thinking about how we can connect with these people, our question should be, What can we do to help these people? not, How can we get these people to help us? Churches seeking to connect with outsiders need constantly to remind themselves that they are doing so for the sake of the outsiders, not for the sake of the church.

Most people have a good sense of when they are being hustled by some organization for its own agenda and when they are being taken seriously for their own sake. They expect to be hustled by the world; they should never feel that way about the church. Our goal is not to be self-serving but rather to adopt servant hearts so that we might be able to offer the best gift of all, Jesus Christ! We want always to remember that we reach out to others as ambassadors of Christ (2 Cor. 5:20).

In working our way through the previous three categories we have begun to put in place a number of things that will prove effective in helping us reach this fourth category as well.

> *Most people have a good sense of when they are being hustled by some organization for its own agenda and when they are being taken seriously for their own sake.*

A congregation that is working to develop a clear and intentional process of discipleship that helps people move from a point of no faith, latent faith, or even comatose faith to a point of enthusiastic discipleship can be certain that it has something of great value to offer.

Within a few minutes' radius of your church, there are people who are wrestling with ultimate questions like, Where have I come from? Why am I here? What is the meaning of life? and What happens when I die? Many of these people might well be interested in a course that helps deal with some of these questions, provided it avoids theological language, makes no assumptions about biblical literacy, and is informal and relational in tone, offering a chance to ask questions, discuss answers, and make friends. Courses on how to read the Bible or how to get started in prayer might receive a good response as well.

Similarly, a church that is on its way to becoming an authentic community, in which the members love and care for one another and genuinely desire for others to join them, can begin to reach out, confident that they are ready to receive company. And a church in which the members are proud to invite their friends and family because they know they will enjoy it is in a good position to think about how to connect with this fourth group in order to invite them, too. Such a church can begin to think about doing so with a sense of real excitement and anticipation.

Who are these people, and what are their needs? What can we do to add value to them and their community? Robert Schuller, founder of the Crystal Cathedral, has said again and again that he built that congregation by following the simple maxim, "Find a need and meet it; find a hurt and heal it."

What are the issues the people in your community are dealing with? If you don't know, it will pay huge dividends to ask. You might consider going door-to-door simply asking the residents what they think these issues are. You might follow up by asking what they think a church interested in helping make this a better community might be able to do. You might ask the same questions of a number of the local social service agencies and the local police. People love to be asked their opinions on important matters and asked to contribute suggestions for how things can be improved. These people will give you a wealth of information if they sense you are serious and not just trying to "make a hit on them" for your church.

In terms of the "middle issues" of living wisely and well, it makes sense that a

> *The best way to raise the profile of your church in your community is to pay attention to the people who live there.*

church that can offer practical help with these issues has a better chance of connecting with outsiders than one that can't. Does your congregation have people who could offer seminars on topics like managing time, stress, or money? Could you sponsor a course or an event related to building stronger marriages, building better homes, parenting for families on the run, taking good care of yourself, recovering from divorce, dealing with loss and grief, or hundreds of other possibilities? Do you have people or connections with people who could help you begin a twelve-step program with a distinctly Christian emphasis?

Such ministries, though offered freely in the spirit of the gospel, bring many benefits back to the church. One is that they open up new opportunities for hands-on, practical ministry by members who are beginning to see themselves as disciples and who are looking for ways to make a difference for Christ. This releases tremendous excitement and enthusiasm into the life of a congregation. Such people are highly likely to be speaking well of their church and inviting others to give it a try. A second benefit is that people in the community, taking note that this is a church that really cares about the community and the people who live here, might well conclude that this church is worth their consideration. This church may notice a gradual increase in the number of walk-in visitors we discussed in chapter 3.

Your Reputation

It is a fact of life that people who have never been in your church and who may not even know any of your members will have formed some impression of you.

Perhaps their impression has been formed simply on the basis of feelings they have experienced while passing your building. Maybe they responded positively to the architecture, or the condition of the lawns, or an amusing sign; maybe they have seen people going in and out who seemed to be happy to be there; or perhaps they have sensed that this is a cold, unfriendly place. But whatever opinion they have formed, and however well founded it may or may not be, chances are they have made comments about it to their friends, and these comments have influenced the way these friends now feel about your church.

I once heard of a pastor who had a number of young couples calling his church to inquire about baptism for their children. Because these people were often strangers to the life of the church they weren't quite sure how to phrase their request and sometimes asked about having their baby "done." This pastor thought it was quite witty in such cases to ask, "How would you like him done: well, medium, or rare?"

That pastor not only lost a lot of good evangelizing opportunities while enjoying his wit but also, in making these young parents feel uncomfortable, undermined the reputation of his church with them and their friends. What is almost a certainty is that they were quickly relating the story of this encounter to neighbors and family, spreading the impression that this was a church to be avoided. Every time the story was told (and chances are it grew with each telling), the reputation of that church would be further diminished.

I am not implying that this pastor should have acceded to every request he received, far from it. But I am saying that in explaining his position he should have been courteous, letting them know that he was taking them very seriously and that he wanted to be of help. People are usually very fragile; they need to be handled with care. It is not asking too much to make sure that people who come into contact with our church for whatever reason are treated with courtesy and grace. We should respond to people as though Jesus himself were in the room witnessing the conversation. Every such encounter offers the opportunity to build a bridge of friendship and grace that Jesus can walk across. Remember that people talk among themselves, sharing their experiences and impressions. Your reputation in the community is a precious asset; take good care of it.

Besides, it would have been much more productive had this pastor and some of the key leaders in the congregation given serious thought to developing a process that could capitalize on the normal inquiries for the so-called rites of passage (baptisms, confirmations, weddings, funerals) from unchurched people and use them as a means of graciously inviting the inquirers to come a little bit closer and find out what this church is all about and what it has to offer.

Your Members' Comments

With everything that we have said so far about the factors affecting the strength of your church's magnetic field, the simple truth remains that, by far, the greatest factor affecting your ability to attract newcomers is the enthusiasm of your current members and their willingness to talk it up in the neighborhood. This single factor outweighs all the others combined.

In fact, it can help overcome weaknesses in the other areas. If your church is in a poor location, members' enthusiasm can overcome this obstacle. If people are saying bad things about your church for some reason and your reputation is taking a hit, enthusiastic members can help to put things right. If your church can't afford an advertising budget, it doesn't cost anything for your members to spread the word.

As a matter of fact, I am not particularly in favor of churches spending a lot of money on advertising. They would usually be better off putting that money and energy into training and encouraging their members to be vocally enthusiastic. On the other hand, where there is good advertising creating a buzz in the community, there is also a good setup for your members to talk about the church. People will be saying things like, "Oh, you go to that church that is sending out the mailings (or the church that sponsors that award, or the church that sent those people around asking about community issues, or offering to pray). Tell me, what is that church really like? Why do you go there? I've been thinking about going to church sometime; maybe I should try that one!"

Summary

In raising your profile the two most important things you can do are create a buzz about your church in the neighborhood and encourage your members to be proactive in talking about it with enthusiasm. Continue to let them know that they are the best ambassadors you have.[1]

The bottom line here is that the more your church has to offer, in terms of its programming and what it adds to the neighborhood, the better chance it has of being able to connect with those who live in the area. This is why it is so impor-

> *In raising your profile the two most important things you can do are create a buzz about your church in the neighborhood and encourage your members to be proactive in talking about it with enthusiasm.*

tant to pay careful attention to everything that has been said in the previous chapters. When your church has developed a solid discipleship training process; carefully thought through how it will welcome and assimilate newcomers; taught its members to speak enthusiastically of the church, of their faith, and to invite others; and actively sought to add value to the community in which it is set by being attentive to its issues and needs, you are well on the way to becoming a magnetic church with a strong attraction for outsiders.

POSTSCRIPT

In chapter 1, I offered three focusing questions, which, I suggested, need to be addressed by any congregation seriously interested in pursuing numerical growth with integrity. As we have considered these questions in the context of the four categories of people every congregation can reach, a couple of things have become abundantly clear. The first is that congregational growth hardly ever happens by accident. Healthy, sustained growth is the result of paying attention to the right things and doing them well, day in and day out, over a long period of time. It is more hard work, dedication, prayer, and commitment than it is glitz and glamour.

The second is that what we have been talking about turns out to involve a lot more than adding a new emphasis to our ministry. There is more to this than simply adding to, or tampering and tinkering with, what we already have. The change required in becoming a church that is able to attract and keep new members from among the currently unchurched amounts to nothing less than changing our spiritual DNA! It requires that we change from the inside out in terms of how we think, what we value, and what it is that drives us. Such radical transformation can never be accomplished by manipulating, coaxing, or nagging. Only God can change the hearts of a congregation, causing the key influencers in that congregation to be willing to change their focus for the sake of connecting with outsiders.

As we have seen, this process of transformation begins with the work of making disciples who absolutely believe that God wants people to come to faith through the ministry of their church, who believe that what they have to offer is worth the effort to share, and who are excited about the possibility of seeing this happen.

We live in an age in which people are spiritually open and curious. Beneath the public veneer of cynicism and materialism, people are quietly longing for truth and for hope. They are hungering and thirsting for spiritual authenticity and reality. On one occasion, Jesus looked at the huge crowds of people who were coming to him for help and thought to himself, "Look at these poor people; they are lost; they are like sheep without a shepherd." Turning to his disciples he said, "The harvest is plentiful but the workers are few. Ask the Lord of the harvest, therefore, to send out workers into his harvest field" (Matt. 9:35-38).

The harvest is every bit as plentiful today as it was when these words were first spoken. The need is still for workers who are willing to go into the fields. For those who do, the challenge is formidable; the work is hard, but the rewards are great, and the joy is indescribable. No one church could ever do everything there is to do about this. But the fact that we can't do everything should never keep us from doing something. And it is a fact that every congregation can do something. Everyone of us can commit to taking the next step!

May your church know the joy of being involved in God's harvest. May many come to know Christ because you are where you are. They will thank you, and they will thank God for you. And your congregation will grow from strength to strength!

APPENDIX 1

The Harvest Bible Study

Matthew 9:35-38

> Jesus went through all the towns and villages, teaching in their synagogues, preaching the good news of the kingdom and healing every disease and sickness. When he saw the crowds, he had compassion on them, because they were harassed and helpless, like sheep without a shepherd. Then he said to his disciples, "The harvest is plentiful but the workers are few. Ask the Lord of the harvest, therefore, to send out workers into his harvest field."

Questions for Reflection on This Passage

1. What do you think Jesus means when he says "the harvest is plentiful"?

2. If Jesus were to spend a day walking through your parish neighborhood, do you think he might say much the same thing? If so, what would he see and hear that might prompt such a comment? If not, what do you think he might say about your parish neighborhood and its opportunities for ministry at the end of the day?

3. In what ways (if any) has the harvest field of your parish neighborhood changed in the past twenty-five years?

4. What kind of church do you think it would take to labor effectively in the harvest field of your parish neighborhood?

5. What are some of the obstacles it might face (a) from the community and (b) from within your church?

6. What are some of the things the harvesters would have to know, or some of the skills they might need, in order to work effectively in your harvest field?

Appendix 2

Becoming a Vital Congregation

Here is an acrostic on the word **vital** that emphasizes some of the key elements influencing congregational vitality.

Visionary leadership. Like it or not, the clergy usually set the tone, temperature, and pace of congregational life. Generally speaking, a congregation cannot go any farther than its leader is able to lead it. In parish life, almost everything rises and falls on leadership. People love to be well led and have great respect for good leadership. In fact, they are frustrated when they are not well led.

Visionary leadership has to do with helping everyone understand why we exist, what we are called to do, why it is important, and what their part could be in carrying out our mission effectively. It has to do with casting a compelling vision that people can see and have a burning desire to buy into; it has to do with stating and restating the basic beliefs, the key purposes, and the core values of the congregation and putting into place a process that will lead to the development of a clear plan of action.

Inspirational worship. In too many places, the tone of our worship is far too somber to engage the spirits of modern people. This does not mean that people have to be entertained; it does require, however, that we acknowledge that they won't stand for boredom.

I believe that we have stressed too much the more cerebral components of liturgy—giving a logical explanation for why the various parts of the liturgy are placed where they are and how it all fits together—at the expense of the equally important issue of how the service makes people feel. I agree with Don Posterski's observation that the people of this generation have hungrier hearts than minds. What people are really looking for in worship is an experience of God, not simply information about God.

Inspirational worship works at the level of the heart, exciting people and arousing in them the desire to be changed and used by God.

Training in discipleship. We have said that making disciples is the primary work of the church. The need to reclaim this ministry at the center of congregational life is one of the key themes of this book. As George Carey, former archbishop of Canterbury, has said so succinctly, "The church that fails to make disciples simply fails."

Authentic community. Unfortunately, we know only too well that a congregation is not necessarily the same as a community. In spite of our stated theology of the church as the people of God, too often we have allowed people to retreat into a kind of individualistic piety that has little room for the life of the faith community. But, it is clear in scripture that the church is called to be a genuine community in which mutual love and care witness to the transforming power of the gospel and bring glory to God.

Loving outreach and evangelism. A healthy congregation is one whose focus is always beyond itself. It understands that it is called to be a city set on a hill, a light shining in the darkness of a broken, self-centered world. It understands further that its witness to the reality of God's kingdom must involve, indeed must combine, good works and clear words. Good works on their own do not explain very much about the gospel; they must be accompanied by a clear explanation of the gospel, which transforms people and helps us to love and to serve.

On the other hand, the words of the gospel alone, separated from a clear and genuine concern for compassion and justice, lack the integrity they need to persuade people to give the gospel a serious hearing. Social care and evangelistic proclamation are, properly understood, a seamless robe. They are distinct, but they should not be separated. When combined, they are a powerful force for transformation.

APPENDIX 3

Helping Your Congregation Thrive

Thriving congregations bring glory to God. They are happy places. They generate excitement, energy, and growth. Here is a list of five suggestions that every church member can follow to help their congregation thrive.

1. Make a Commitment to Growth. The New Testament is clear that all who become followers of Jesus are called to grow toward spiritual maturity. A static faith is a boring faith; the adventure and excitement of Christian living are all in the growth. This growth is called discipleship. The goal of discipleship is to become ever more like Jesus in thought, character, and behavior. Discipleship involves getting to know God better in a personal way. It calls us to a broader understanding of God's purposes so that we might be able to serve and represent God more faithfully in the world and in the church. There is enough here to keep all of us actively engaged in this exciting adventure for the rest of our lives!

2. Make a Commitment to Welcome. As much as it depends on you, make sure that your congregation is a warm and welcoming place for newcomers. Horror stories abound of people feeling ignored and unwelcome when they attend a new church. This is not because the members of these "cold" churches are uncaring or unfeeling. Usually it is just an oversight. Good people, caught up in the warmth and enjoyment of spending time with their long-standing friends at church, simply overlook the newcomer standing there feeling awkward and strange. While greeting your friends, keep one eye open for newcomers whom you can welcome; greet them as though they are the personal guests of Jesus; show interest in them; introduce them to your friends; invite them back. You never know what might have brought this person to church on this particular morning. A church will never be any better than the welcome it gives to visitors.

3. Make a Commitment to Ministry. As much as you can, offer your gifts of time and talent to help the ministry of your church thrive. For many of us, time is our most valuable resource and there are many demands made on it. Time offered to the ministry of the church is a precious gift. All of us have gifts and talents that can be used in effective ministry. When we know what these talents are and how they can be used, it makes the time we give more effective.

4. Make a Commitment to Generosity. Remember that ministry costs money and that good ministry costs even more money. Growing disciples are learning the importance of financial generosity for both their personal growth and the support of their church's ministry. The key question here is not, How much must I give? but rather, How much can I give? There is great fulfillment and pleasure in generosity because this is how God designed us.

5. Make a Commitment to Invite. We live in a hurting world that badly needs to hear and experience the good news of God's graciousness to us in Jesus Christ. Most of us have well-developed spheres of influence among neighbors, family, and friends, within which we can share what our faith means to us and invite them to come with us to sample the life of our church community. We are surrounded by people who are simply waiting for the invitation.

NOTES

1. Thinking About Growth

1. For a fuller discussion of the gospel under the headings "reconciliation, reign, and response" see Harold Percy, *Good News People: An Introduction to Evangelism for Tongue-Tied Christians*, chaps. 2 and 3 (Toronto: Anglican Book Centre, 1996).

2. See Matthew 9:35-38 and 28:16-20. For a more detailed discussion of the rationale for evangelism see *Good News People*, chap. 1.

3. Loren B. Mead, *More Than Numbers: The Way Churches Grow* (Washington, D.C.: Alban Institute, 1993).

4. Rick Warren, *The Purpose-Driven Church: Growth Without Compromising Your Message and Mission* (Grand Rapids, Mich.: Zondervan, 1995), p. 188.

2. Those in the Pews

1. Rick Warren, *The Purpose-Driven Church: Growth Without Compromising Your Message and Mission* (Grand Rapids, Mich.: Zondervan, 1995), p. 50.

2. For a discussion of Christendom and its waning influence, see Loren B. Mead, *The Once and Future Church: Reinventing the Congregation for a New Mission Frontier* (Washington D.C.: Alban Institute, 1991).

3. For practical help in teaching some of the key issues of discipleship, see Harold Percy, *Following Jesus: First Steps on the Way* (Toronto: Anglican Book Centre, 1993).

4. For a fuller discussion of the three dimensions of discipleship, see Harold Percy, *Good News People: An Introduction to Evangelism for Tongue-Tied Christians* (Toronto: Anglican Book Centre, 1996), pp. 44-54.

3. Those Who Walk In

1. George G. Hunter III, *The Celtic Way of Evangelism: How Christianity Can Reach the West . . . Again* (Nashville: Abingdon, 2000), p. 117.

2. Howard Hanchey, *Church Growth and the Power of Evangelism* (Cambridge, Mass.: Cowley Publications, 1990).

3. For more on welcoming and assimilating newcomers see Andrew D. Weeks, *Welcome! Tools and Techniques for New Member Ministry* (Washington, D.C.: Alban Institute, 1992) and Roy M. Oswald and Speed B. Leas, *The Inviting Church: A Study of New Member Assimilation* (Washington, D.C.: Alban Institute, 1987).

4. This four-session course is available on video, along with guidelines for course and discussion leaders through Trinity Anglican Church, Streetsville, Ontario. Phone (905) 826-1901, or email shirley@trinitystreetsville.org.

4. Friends and Family of Members

1. For a more detailed discussion of intimidation in evangelism, see chap. 4 of my *Good News People: An Introduction to Evangelism for Tongue-Tied Christians* (Toronto: Anglican Book Centre, 1996).

2. For more on this see *Good News People*, chaps. 6–8.

3. Geoffrey Willis, *Won by One: Helping Your Friends Find Faith* (London: Marshall Pickering, 1994), p. x.

4. For more on the culture barrier see George G. Hunter III, *Church for the Unchurched* (Nashville: Abingdon, 1996), pp. 59-67.

5. For an excellent and very important explanation and discussion of "the middle issues," in relation to Hiebert's article, "The Flaw of the Excluded Middle," see George G. Hunter III, *The Celtic Way of Evangelism: How Christianity Can Reach the West . . . Again* (Nashville: Abingdon, 2000), pp. 30-35.

5. Those Who Live in the Neighborhood

1. For an innovative and insightful comparison between restaurants and churches, see Russ Chandler, *Feeding the Flock: Restaurants and Churches You'd Stand in Line For* (Washington, D.C.: Alban Institute, 1998).